T0309268

ETHICS TRAINING FOR MANAGERS

Can employees be trained to make more ethical decisions? If so, how? Providing evidence-based and practical answers to these critical questions is the purpose of this book. To answer these questions, the authors—four organizational psychologists who specialize in the study of ethical decision making—translate insights based on decades of scientific research. Whether you are a student, educator, HR manager, compliance professional, or simply someone interested in the topic of ethics education, this book offers a road map for designing ethics training programs that work.

Logan L. Watts, Ph.D. is an Assistant Professor in the Department of Psychology at Baruch College and the Graduate Center, CUNY. He has published extensively on the topic of ethics education and formerly managed an ethics training program for early-career professionals.

Kelsey E. Medeiros, Ph.D. is an Assistant Professor of Management at the University of Nebraska Omaha. Her research focuses on workplace trouble-makers, including those who act unethically. She has published over 30 articles on troublemakers and consults with organizations on related topics.

Tristan J. McIntosh, Ph.D. is a faculty member at Washington University in St. Louis where she researches ethical, professional, and social issues that arise in research, medical, and organizational settings. She is also a co-founder and ethics consultant at Ethics Advantage, LLC.

Tyler J. Mulhearn, Ph.D. is an I/O Psychologist at Neurostat Analytical Solutions, LLC. He received his Ph.D. in Industrial and Organizational Psychology at the University of Oklahoma. His research has been published in *Science and Engineering Ethics, Accountability in Research,* and *Creativity Research Journal.*

Giving Voice to Values

Series Editor: Mary C. Gentile

The *Giving Voice to Values* series is a collection of books on Business Ethics and Corporate Social Responsibility that brings a practical, solutions-oriented, skill-building approach to the salient questions of values-driven leadership.

Giving Voice to Values (GVV: www.GivingVoiceToValues.org)—the curriculum, the pedagogy, and the research upon which it is based—was designed to transform the foundational assumptions upon which the teaching of business ethics is based, and importantly, to equip future business leaders to know not only what is right—but how to make it happen.

ETHICS TRAINING FOR MANAGERS

Best Practices and Techniques

Logan L. Watts, Kelsey E. Medeiros, Tristan J. McIntosh, and Tyler J. Mulhearn

Routledge
Taylor & Francis Group

LONDON AND NEW YORK

First published 2021
by Routledge
2 Park Square, Milton Park, Abingdon, Oxon OX14 4RN

and by Routledge
52 Vanderbilt Avenue, New York, NY 10017

Routledge is an imprint of the Taylor & Francis Group, an informa business

British Library Cataloguing-in-Publication Data
A catalogue record for this book is available from the British Library

Library of Congress Cataloging-in-Publication Data
A catalog record for this book has been requested

ISBN: 978-0-367-24267-1 (hbk)
ISBN: 978-0-367-24266-4 (pbk)
ISBN: 978-0-429-28143-3 (ebk)

Typeset in Joanna
by MPS Limited, Dehradun

CONTENTS

ACKNOWLEDGMENTS

This book would not have been possible without the generous support, expertise, and efforts of so many people. First and foremost, we must begin by thanking our colleagues in the Department of Psychology at the University of Oklahoma (OU) who taught us just about everything we know about the science of ethics training. During our time as doctoral students at OU, we had the privilege of working under two of the world's eminent scholars in this area, Mike Mumford and Shane Connelly. Additionally, we must thank our fellow doctoral students who conducted ethics research with us while at OU, including Zhanna Bagdasarov, Alexandra MacDougall, James Johnson, Jensen Mecca, Carter Gibson, Vince Giorgini, Paul Partlow, Logan Steele, Michelle Todd, Cory Higgs, Brett Torrence, and Megan Turner. We are also grateful for the efforts of the many doctoral students and faculty who contributed to ethics research at OU before our time. Each of these researchers helped pave the way for the practical insights presented in this book.

Second, we must acknowledge the patience and efforts of our editorial team. To Mary Gentile, thank you for the opportunity to contribute to the Giving Voice to Values (GVV) series. For us, the opportunity to translate practical insights emerging from research on ethics training and education is a dream come true. To Rebecca Marsh, thank you for your encouragement and guidance throughout the publication process. In facilitating an early review of our book proposal by external experts, you helped us identify important areas for improvement. Thanks to Sophie Peoples and Neema Lama who answered many of our questions and facilitated the production process. To Alessa Natale, thank you for serving as our in-house reviewer, including editing and formatting the work of four authors with varying voices and writing styles—no easy task! Thanks to our friends and family members who read earlier drafts of the book. You helped stretch our research translation skills by calling out technical jargon and adding clarity. Of course, the opinions stated in this book, and any errors, are our own.

Third, thank you to the Eugene M. Lang Junior Faculty Research Fellowship Program at Baruch College, CUNY. The Lang Program provided a small grant which helped fund the editing and formatting of this book. In addition, the Department of Psychology at Baruch College enabled one of the authors to take a semester off from teaching while working on the book. We are grateful for such supportive colleagues.

Fourth, and finally, we must thank the many scholars coming before us who contributed to the research cited in this book. It would take too long to acknowledge each of these scholars by name here. However, their names can be found in the references listed at the end of each chapter. It goes without saying that a book like this—which focuses on translating scientific research on ethics training for applied audiences—would not have been possible without your efforts.

June 22, 2020

INTRODUCTION

Is it possible to train adults to be more ethical? This is a question that we have asked our students and audiences for years with mixed responses. Perhaps the most common response is silence accompanied by a furrowed brow. Of course, hesitation of this kind is rational when one is presented with a loaded question. How a person answers this question reveals a number of consequential assumptions about how they view the world.

For example, is the world made up of 'good' and 'bad' people, or are all of us capable of making unethical decisions? Decades of research in psychology and the social sciences suggest that the latter assumption is a more accurate explanation for how most human beings actually behave. Indeed, most people want to do the 'right thing.' Yet, their decisions do not always match their intentions. This does not make these individuals bad or evil. Rather, it just means they are human.

Readers of this book probably already believe that adults can be trained to be more ethical. Otherwise, why read an instruction manual on designing ethics training? Our readers, like us, probably also believe that ethics is critical to the healthy functioning of organizations. Nevertheless, we cannot assume everyone holds these assumptions. Throughout the course of this book, we will provide scientific evidence for the effectiveness of ethics training and its role in increasing organizational functioning.

Part I of this book is dedicated to making the case for the value of ethics training programs, as well as ethics more broadly, in organizations. This information may be especially beneficial for readers who are tasked with influencing managers and coworkers that ethics interventions, such as training, are worth the investment.

Part II provides guidance on how to map out and make decisions about the key elements that make up any ethics training program. For example, we devote chapters to topics like planning, identifying useful content, selecting engaging delivery methods, and evaluating program effectiveness.

Finally, in Part III we address practical concerns that arise when implementing ethics training programs in organizations. These chapters can guide readers on how to pilot test a new ethics training program to iron out any kinks as well as how to monitor changes in the environment to ensure that training content remains relevant. Part III also provides recommendations for managing the training environment. The final chapter presents guidelines for implementing ethics training programs in cross-cultural contexts.

It should be clear from these brief chapter descriptions that designing and implementing an effective ethics training program is no simple task. This book provides a road map showing many tried and true routes for managing an effective program. However, none of these routes are easy, and hundreds of important judgment calls are required along the way. If the journey ever seems insurmountable, don't hesitate to reach out for help from ethics training experts. Just as a map is more useful in the hands of an experienced navigator, so too this book will be more useful to managers who partner with experts in this domain.

To answer our opening question, yes, it is possible to train adults to be more ethical. The goal of this book is to show you how. By the end of this book, the reader should have a better understanding of the importance of ethics training and how to develop and manage an effective ethics training program. After all, it is possible to train adults to be more ethical, but how the training is planned, executed, and maintained can make all the difference between a subpar and an exceptional program. We hope the reader can harness the insights provided in this book to manage their own exceptional ethics training program.

PART I

WHY INVEST IN ETHICS TRAINING?

1

WHY ETHICS IN BUSINESS MATTERS

Logan L. Watts

***

In the past, ethics has often been viewed as a 'nice to have,' rather than a 'must have,' aspect of success in business. Some managers believe that ethics and profits are competing priorities. Others may think that ethics and business performance are independent issues. However, these ideas are misconceptions. In fact, a large body of research shows that ethics is fundamental to organizational success (Sisodia, Wolfe, & Sheth, 2003). In other words, ethics is critical to a firm's competitive advantage. Most of the evidence for this conclusion stems from case studies and survey studies. The goal of this chapter is to summarize this evidence.

Evidence from case studies

Ethics seminars routinely use case studies of corporate scandals to illustrate the value of business ethics. This is for good reason. Case studies provide memorable examples of ethical issues and the potential consequences of poor decisions. Classic examples include Enron and Madoff Investments. In both cases, widespread financial fraud ruined multibillion dollar firms. Here we focus on three more recent cases. Each case demonstrates that business ethics—or the lack thereof—has important implications for organizational success.

The three scandals summarized here share an underlying pattern. This pattern involves the breakdown of relationships with stakeholders. Stakeholders are 'persons or groups that have, or claim, ownership, rights, or interests in a corporation and its activities, past, present, or future' (Clarkson, 1995, p. 106). In other words, stakeholders are parties that organizations need in order to function and thrive. Example stakeholders include shareholders, employees, customers, suppliers, community members, government agencies, special interest groups, and even the environment (Freeman, Harrison, Wicks, Parmar, & De Colle, 2010).

The goal of ethical standards, as well as legal regulations, is to protect the rights and interests of stakeholders. Organizational misconduct occurs when employees act in ways that violate these standards. Such misconduct may occur intentionally (e.g., corruption) or unintentionally (e.g., neglect). Regardless of intentions, organizational misconduct harms relationships with one or more stakeholder groups. This is because misconduct compromises the trust between parties that is needed for relationships to function. To illustrate these ideas, next we describe corporate scandals at Volkswagen, Wells Fargo, and Facebook.

Emissions scandal at Volkswagen

In 2015, the Environmental Protection Agency issued a notice of violation to Volkswagen. The notice accused the company of installing 'defeat devices' on close to half a million vehicles sold in the USA since 2009. This device temporarily suppressed nitrogen oxide—a poisonous gas—just long enough to pass emissions tests. Passing these tests allowed the company to *appear* to comply with US and European air quality standards. The reality, however, was a different story. Once the vehicles were on the road, the defeat device shut off in order to improve driving performance. This practice pushed vehicle emissions far above regulatory standards. Investigations later proved that over two dozen company executives had been aware of this deception for years (Cavico & Mujtaba, 2016).

Through these actions, Volkswagen abused multiple stakeholders. First, the company took advantage of customers by engaging in deceptive advertising. Second, the company harmed its relationship with government agencies around the world. Third, any investor holding stock in Volkswagen experienced a severe decline in the value of their holdings. Fourth, the environment and the public at large suffered from elevated emissions levels. One study estimated the excess pollution would result in over 50 premature deaths as well as nonfatal health issues for many others (Barrett, 2015).

Following the scandal, the consequences for Volkswagen have been severe. The CEO and other executives were forced to resign. The company announced a worldwide recall of 11 million vehicles. Governments and automakers around the world launched investigations into the company. In 2018, Volkswagen agreed to pay over $2 billion in fines to the US government alone (Thaler, Herbst, & Merz, 2018). At a minimum, the emissions scandal at Volkswagen shows that unethical business practices can severely disrupt organizational operations.

Fake accounts scandal at Wells Fargo

In 2016, Wells Fargo was accused of opening two million fake accounts. These accounts were opened on behalf of customers without their knowledge. Executives initially reacted by minimizing the problem. For example, senior managers suggested the 'few bad apples' involved had already been fired. However, follow-up investigations revealed that the issues were systemic (Tayan, 2019). Branch managers reported that sales goals set by senior managers were unrealistic. Instead of inspiring higher performance, the ambitious goals encouraged employees to cut corners. Some managers even trained their employees on how to open fake accounts to boost branch metrics. In response to pressure from Congress and the media, CEO John Stumpf resigned. In a company-wide statement, the new CEO Tim Sloan admitted to the pervasive nature of the problem:

> Despite our ongoing efforts to combat these unacceptable bad practices and bad behaviors, they persisted, because we either minimized the problem, or we failed to see the problem for what it really was—something bigger than we originally imagined. (Independent Directors, 2017, p. 59)

Following the scandal, a number of consequences have emerged for Wells Fargo and its stakeholders. The company was ordered to pay $185 million in fines. It also spent hundreds of millions of dollars auditing its sales practices and engaging in public relations campaigns to restore its reputation. Share prices declined. Customers' finances and credit histories were negatively impacted. Over 5,000 employees lost their jobs. Interviews with former managers showed that the unrealistic sales targets contributed to a stressful workplace—one of the leading causes of employee illness and fatalities (Beehr, 1995).

Finally, we should not overlook the potential indirect consequences on the broader public. When the reputation of a global banking institution is harmed, confidence in the entire economic system suffers. Following the Great Recession, trust in financial institutions was at an all-time low (Stevenson & Wolfers, 2011). The Wells Fargo scandal contributed to further distrust of banks, and economic instability, at an already uncertain time.

Data privacy scandal at Facebook

In 2018, the public learned that Facebook committed a massive violation of their users' data privacy rights. The company admitted to sharing the personal data of 87 million users with a consulting firm named Cambridge Analytica, without these users' permission.

It is important to consider how this data scandal occurred. When Facebook users agreed to the fine print to use some third-party applications, they agreed to share data from their profiles. These users didn't know, however, that in agreeing to share their own data they were also agreeing to share the data of their personal connections (i.e., 'friends') who never agreed to the arrangement. To make matters worse, Cambridge Analytica used these data to target users with advertisements with the goal of influencing government elections in the USA and around the globe (Meredith, 2018).

Rather than being a case of intentional abuse, it appears that Facebook's misconduct mainly resulted from neglect. Executives failed to anticipate how their technology and systems could be exploited by third parties. In CEO Mark Zuckerberg's testimony before Congress, he stated that Facebook executives 'didn't do enough to prevent these tools from being used for harm' and that 'we didn't take a broad enough view of our responsibility' (Zuckerberg, 2018).

At the time of this writing, the consequences of the Facebook scandal are still developing. Of course, the company's users—particularly those whose data were collected without their permission—were the primary victims. Facebook's stock price also declined in the weeks following the scandal (Peruzzi, Zollo, Quattrociocchi, & Scala, 2018). Long-term consequences for Facebook and the industry remain to be seen as leaders around the world debate how to effectively regulate technology companies.

To summarize, case studies of ethical scandals demonstrate the negative consequences of misconduct on an organization's operations and reputation. While the three examples highlighted here are from Global Fortune 500 firms, many examples can also be found in public sector and nonprofit organizations of all sizes. Organizations differ in terms of their mission and strategic objectives. Yet, the ability of each organization to deliver on its mission rests on strong relationships with stakeholders—relationships that are compromised by unethical behavior.

Evidence from survey studies

Survey research provides another lens for viewing the link between organizational ethics and success. Survey studies are useful because they allow researchers to estimate statistical relationships (i.e., correlations) between ethics and key metrics of organizational success. In addition, survey studies include large samples with many hundreds of organizations. With large sample sizes, we can be more confident that the results are trustworthy and applicable to other organizations.

Measuring organizational ethics

In order to appreciate evidence from survey studies, it is first important to understand how researchers measure organizational ethics. When researchers study organizational ethics, they typically do so by asking respondents how ethical they perceive an organization and its practices to be. Survey respondents can be customers, shareholders, industry experts, or more commonly, the organization's own employees.

In designing these surveys, researchers must first identify a set of questions or statements that represent the types of behaviors one might expect to see in an ethical organization. Next, researchers must decide on a rating scale. Rating scales provide a way to quantify respondents' perceptions. In other words, rating scales transform respondents' perceptions into numbers. Once perceptions are quantified, researchers can analyze these data using statistics. Table 1.1 presents an example rating scale with some survey questions for illustrative purposes.

Table 1.1 Example Survey Rating Scale for Measuring Organizational Ethics

Instructions: Using a 5-point rating scale, rate how strongly you agree or disagree with the following statements based on your experiences working at Company X.

Rating scale:	1	2	3	4	5
	Strongly disagree	Somewhat disagree	Neither disagree nor agree	Somewhat agree	Strongly agree

____ The company treats employees and customers with respect.

____ Managers take the company code of ethics seriously.

____ Employees feel safe to voice their concerns about ethical issues.

____ Managers talk about the importance of upholding ethical values.

____ Supervisors are role models of ethical behavior.

____ There are clear systems in place for reporting ethical issues.

____ The company responds quickly and effectively to ethical issues.

Note. This table is presented for illustrative purposes only. We encourage readers interested in application to use validated scales for measuring perceptions of organizational ethics, of which there are several options (e.g., Cullen, Victor, & Bronson, 1993; Jondle, Ardichvili, & Mitchell, 2014; Kaptein, 2008).

Survey researchers also collect information on metrics of organizational success. For example, employee job satisfaction, turnover rates, and customer loyalty ratings are all potentially important metrics to consider. Further, researchers can collect financial metrics like revenue growth, profitability, and return on assets. With this information, researchers can test whether there is a link between respondents' perceptions of organizational ethics and metrics of organizational success.

There are two important assumptions underlying survey research on this topic. First, measuring organizational ethics is about perception. An organization is classified as more or less ethical, relative to other organizations, depending on how respondents perceive it. Second, organizational ethics is viewed as a continuum. Rather than being a black-or-white, yes-or-no issue, organizational ethics can hypothetically range from egregiously corrupt to squeaky clean. Of course, perceptions of organizational ethics usually fall somewhere between these extremes.

In other words, survey researchers define organizational ethics as the extent to which respondents perceive an organization to be ethical. Of course, we might trust some respondents' perceptions more than others. For example, respondents who have many opportunities to observe the organization's practices up close are likely to provide more accurate information. Also, it helps if respondents are motivated to provide their honest opinions. Finally, we can place more stock in the information provided by respondents if they agree with one another. Now that we have covered how survey research on ethics is conducted, we turn to summarizing the evidence from this research concerning the link between ethics and organizational success.

Organizational ethics and success

There is now broad consensus among researchers that organizational ethics is positively related to (i.e., correlated with) many markers of organizational success. Although correlation does not always equal causation, the best available evidence suggests that ethics is positively related to how effectively an organization functions as well as economic growth. This means that as organizations become more ethical, we can expect them to perform at higher levels. This also means that as organizations become less ethical, we can expect their effectiveness to suffer.

Given that hundreds of studies have examined the link between organizational ethics and performance (Margolis, Elfenbein, & Walsh, 2009), it is beyond the scope of this chapter to review this body of work in detail. However, we selected two highly cited research studies conducted by Dr. Curtis Verschoor, a research professor in the School of Accounting at DePaul University, to present as illustrative examples. These two studies provide a glimpse into survey research on this topic.

In 1997, Business Week published a ranking of Fortune 500 companies based on eight objective performance metrics reported annually over a 3-year period. Professor Verschoor reviewed annual statements by these companies and found that only 27% of them explicitly referred to their commitment to ethical standards. Examples of companies that consistently stated their commitment to ethics in their annual reports included Johnson & Johnson, Du Pont, and IBM (Verschoor, 1998). Next, he compared these data with the performance rankings of the firms published in Business Week. Verschoor found that companies that explicitly mentioned their commitment to ethics were ranked significantly higher—14 percentiles higher—than those who did not in terms of performance.

In another study of the Fortune 500 published the following year, Verschoor (1999) found that companies committed to upholding ethical standards also had stronger reputations in their industries. This study compared companies based on external rankings of corporate reputation—the 'most admired' large companies. These rankings were based on thousands of industry expert ratings collected by Fortune. Verschoor found that the reputation rankings of companies that included explicit statements about their commitment to upholding ethical standards were, on average, five percentiles higher than those that did not verbalize such a commitment.

The findings of these studies point to a clear conclusion: Ethics and success are positively correlated. Companies that pay more attention to ethics tend to outperform their competitors financially, and they also have stronger reputations in their industries. Put simply, ethical organizations have a competitive advantage.

Why ethics is good for business

The two studies just reviewed help establish that organizational ethics is positively related to success. However, this research does not explain why this link exists. We can speculate about many potential reasons why ethics is good for business. For example, organizational ethics may lead to:

- Increased employee productivity, job satisfaction, and organizational commitment
- Decreased employee turnover and instances of counterproductive work behavior (e.g., employee theft, unnecessary absences, harassment, drug abuse)
- Increased customer satisfaction, retention, and engagement
- Improved relations with investors, suppliers, distributors, and regulatory bodies
- Positive media coverage that bolsters reputation and attracts new talent
- Supporting the health of the planet in ways that enable long-term growth

Researchers all over the world have investigated some of these explanations using survey studies. One study of HR managers working at 164 companies listed on the Stock Exchange of Thailand found that companies with stronger ethical cultures demonstrated higher levels of job satisfaction, organizational commitment, and team spirit among employees (Koonmee, Singhapakdi, Virakul, & Lee, 2010). In other words, employees who work for ethical organizations tend to be more engaged. Engaged employees are more productive and stay at their jobs longer, contributing directly to the bottom line (Halbesleben & Wheeler, 2008). Thus, one way ethics promotes success is by strengthening the organization's relationship with its employees.

Another study of 3,821 professionals working in 130 companies in South Korea found that employees working for more ethical organizations reported higher levels of commitment and a greater willingness to help their coworkers (Chun, Shin, Choi, & Kim, 2013). Thus, another way that organizational ethics boosts performance is by promoting a spirit of collegiality and teamwork among employees.

The competitive advantage gained by organizational ethics is not limited to positive effects on employees, however. In a study of 150 Indian manufacturing firms, researchers found that corporate initiatives aimed at strengthening relationships with other stakeholder groups—including customers, investors, suppliers, the community, and the environment—were also positively correlated with organizational performance (Mishra & Suar, 2010).

To summarize, ethics is good for business because ethical companies have strong relationships with stakeholders. Employees who trust and respect their organizations are more motivated and committed to their work. Customers who trust the source of their products and services are more likely to become repeat buyers. Shareholders who believe a firm's managers are operating as trustworthy stewards of their investments are more likely stay invested. When we add up the benefits of these strong stakeholder relationships, it is easy to see how ethics is a critical resource that promotes organizational success.

Conclusion

Based on case studies and survey research, it is clear that ethics is fundamental to an organization's competitive advantage. The essence of business ethics is maintaining and building trusting relationships with stakeholders. In fact, one of the fastest ways to derail a company is to ignore the needs of a key stakeholder group.

Due to rapid changes in technology and other factors, managers today must be especially strategic to help their organization expand or even maintain market share (Watts, Patel, Rothstein, & Natale, 2020). In response to these conditions, companies are like high-speed trains (see Figure 1.1) racing against their competitors along a perpetual bridge toward some uncertain, but (hopefully) brighter future. Columns representing the firm's relationships with its key stakeholders support this bridge. The integrity of the bridge, and the success of the train in reaching its destination, ultimately depends upon the strength of these stakeholder relationships. Thus, abusing or ignoring the interests of any key stakeholder group can expose a company to substantial risk.

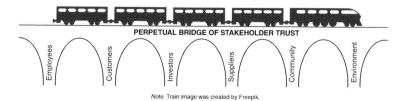

Note. Train image was created by Freepik.

Figure 1.1 Perpetual Bridge of Stakeholder Trust.

The goal of ethics programs, such as ethics training, is to help employees learn to make decisions that inspire trust from stakeholders—decisions that maintain and strengthen the columns supporting the bridge. Thus, it is useful to think of managers of ethics programs as the engineers tasked with assessing, maintaining, and improving the structural integrity of the bridge over time. Although your organization may not have a formal position designated as the 'ethics training manager,' we use the term broadly throughout this book to refer to any professional who is responsible for designing, implementing, or monitoring an ethics training program in their organization. Ethics training represents one tool among many for promoting organizational ethics, strengthening relationships with stakeholders, and securing a competitive advantage.

Now that we have made the case for the importance of ethics to organizational success, our next task is to address how people arrive at ethical decisions. Why do some employees make unethical decisions while others choose 'the right path?' Ethical dilemmas are not always 'black or white.' Our world is complex. Clear rules are not always available to guide employees through every potential situation. Even when there are clear rules, employees do not always follow them. In the next chapter, we present insights from decades of research in psychology explaining when and why people make good versus bad decisions at work. Knowledge of this research can help improve the likelihood of delivering effective ethics training programs.

References

Barrett, S. R. H. (2015). Impact of the Volkswagen emissions control defeat device on US public health. *Environmental Research Letters, 10*, 114005. doi:10.1088/1748-9326/10/11/114005.

Beehr, T. A. (1995). *Psychological stress in the workplace.* New York, NY: Routledge.

Cavico, F. J., & Mujtaba, B. G. (2016). Volkswagen emissions scandal: A global case study of legal, ethical, and practical consequences and recommendations for sustainable management. *Global Journal of Research in Business & Management, 4*, 303–311.

Chun, J. S., Shin, Y., Choi, J. N., & Kim, M. S. (2013). How does corporate ethics contribute to firm financial performance? The mediating role of collective organizational commitment and organizational citizenship behavior. *Journal of Management, 39*, 853–877.

Clarkson, M. E. (1995). A stakeholder framework for analyzing and evaluating corporate social performance. *Academy of Management Review, 20*, 92–117.

Cullen, J. B., Victor, B., & Bronson, J. W. (1993). The ethical climate questionnaire: An assessment of its development and validity. *Psychological Reports, 73*, 667–674.

Freeman, R. E., Harrison, J. S., Wicks, A. C., Parmar, B. L., & De Colle, S. (2010). *Stakeholder theory: The state of the art.* Cambridge, UK: Cambridge University Press.

Halbesleben, J. R., & Wheeler, A. R. (2008). The relative roles of engagement and embeddedness in predicting job performance and intention to leave. *Work & Stress, 22*, 242–256.

Independent Directors of the Board of Wells Fargo & Company (2017). *Sales practices investigation report.* Retrieved on April 25, 2017 from https://www08.wellsfargomedia.com/assets/pdf/about/investor-relations/presentations/2017/board-report.pdf.

Jondle, D., Ardichvili, A., & Mitchell, J. (2014). Modeling ethical business culture: Development of the ethical business culture survey and its use to validate the CEBC model of ethical business culture. *Journal of Business Ethics, 119*, 29–43.

Kaptein, M. (2008). Developing and testing a measure for the ethical culture of organizations: The corporate ethical virtues model. *Journal of Organizational Behavior, 29*, 923–947.

Koonmee, K., Singhapakdi, A., Virakul, B., & Lee, D. J. (2010). Ethics institutionalization, quality of work life, and employee job-related outcomes: A survey of human resource managers in Thailand. *Journal of Business Research, 63*, 20–26.

Margolis, J. D., Elfenbein, H. A., & Walsh, J. P. (2009). Does it pay to be good...and does it matter? A meta-analysis of the relationship between corporate social and financial performance. *SSRN*, 1–68. doi:10.2139/ssrn.1866371.

Meredith, S. (2018, April 10). Facebook-Cambridge Analytica: A timeline of the data hijacking scandal. Retrieved December 14, 2018 from https://www.cnbc.com/2018/04/10/facebook-cambridge-analytica-a-timeline-of-the-data-hijacking-scandal.html.

Mishra, S., & Suar, D. (2010). Does corporate social responsibility influence firm performance of Indian companies? *Journal of Business Ethics*, 95, 571–601.

Peruzzi, A., Zollo, F., Quattrociocchi, W., & Scala, A. (2018). How news may affect markets' complex structure: The case of Cambridge Analytica. *Entropy*, 20, 765–776.

Sisodia, R., Wolfe, D., & Sheth, J. N. (2003). *Firms of endearment: How world-class companies profit from passion and purpose.* Upper Saddle River, NJ: Pearson Prentice Hall.

Stevenson, B., & Wolfers, J. (2011). Trust in public institutions over the business cycle. *American Economic Review*, 101, 281–287.

Tayan, B. (2019). The Wells Fargo cross-selling scandal. *Stanford Closer Look Series*, 62, 1–14.

Thaler, V. S., Herbst, U., & Merz, M. A. (2018). A real product scandal's impact on a high-equity brand: A new approach to assessing scandal impact. *Journal of Product & Brand Management*, 27, 427–439.

Verschoor, C. C. (1998). A study of the link between a corporation's financial performance and its commitment to ethics. *Journal of Business Ethics*, 17, 1509–1516.

Verschoor, C. C. (1999). Corporate performance is closely linked to a strong ethical commitment. *Business and Society Review*, 104, 407–415.

Watts, L. L., Patel, K. R., Rothstein, E. G., & Natale, A. N. (2020). How do leaders plan for firm innovation? Strategic planning processes and constraints. In M. D. Mumford & E. M. Todd (Eds.), *Creativity and innovation in organizations*, 243–270. New York, NY: Routledge.

Zuckerberg, M. (2018, April 10). *Hearing before the United States Senate Committee on the Judiciary and the United States Senate Committee on Commerce, Science and Transportation*. Retrieved August 31, 2019 from https://www.judiciary.senate.gov/imo/media/doc/04-10-18%20Zuckerberg%20Testimony.pdf.

2

ETHICAL DECISION MAKING

Logan L. Watts Ph.D.

***

Everyone has faced situations in which deciding on the 'right' course of action is not entirely clear. Further, even if you know what the 'right' decision is, this does not guarantee that you will effectively follow through on it. Managers face ethically loaded problems on a routine basis. Consider, for example, the following dilemmas:

- Should you suspend your highest-selling employee for engaging in sales practices that violate the organization's code of conduct? And if so, how can this decision be carried out?
- Should you invest resources in new manufacturing processes that are better for the environment if the current processes already meet legal requirements? And if so, how can you go about securing support from senior leaders for this plan?
- Should you report a fellow manager who is engaged in an intimate relationship with a subordinate even if both parties are 'keeping it

professional' at work? And if so, what steps can you take to effectively implement this decision?

The purpose of this chapter is to clarify what an ethical decision is and describe the mental processes that help people identify and act on ethical decisions. Additionally, we summarize research on psychological factors and organizational factors that impact the odds that people will make ethical decisions at work.

Key terms

It has been said that attempting to define ethics is 'like nailing jello to a wall' (Lewis, 1985, p. 377). However, any useful discussion of ethical decision making must begin with some clarification on what exactly an *ethical decision* is. It is important to note up front that not all researchers agree on this subject. This book will not explore every major viewpoint about ethics in detail (see Forsyth, 1980). Instead, we draw primarily on perspectives from psychological science to offer an overview of ethical decision making in the context of organizations.

The 3 C's of ethical decision making

Ethical decision making is the process of generating and implementing ethical decisions. Ethical decisions tend to uphold legal and professional standards and show respect for relevant stakeholders (DuBois, 2008). Stakeholders may include coworkers, supervisors, subordinates, customers, investors, or even society more generally. To understand how ethical decision making occurs, it is first important to define what an ethical decision is. A decision can be considered ethical if it satisfies three basic principles, including: (i) compliance, (ii) consensus, and (iii) consequences. We refer to these principles as the 3 C's of ethical decision making. These principles apply not only to the content of the decision itself but also to how the decision is implemented.

The first principle, compliance, suggests that a decision is ethical if it *complies* with explicit rules. Rules refer to organizational policies, industry standards, or legal regulations. Second, according to the principle of consensus, a decision is ethical if the majority of members within one's society view the decision as ethical. We use the term *consensus* to refer to implicit rules (e.g., values) that guide individual behavior in socially acceptable ways. Third, the principle of consequences holds that a decision is ethical if it maximizes benefits, and minimizes harm, to the greatest number of people. When any action is taken that satisfies all three of these principles, we can be more confident that the action is ethical.

Satisfying the 3 C's may appear simple on the surface. However, when applying these principles in the 'real world,' it becomes clear that determining whether a decision is ethical, and translating this decision into ethical action, is not always a straightforward process. Each principle has its own limitations. Even if an ethical solution is identified based on the 3 C's, this does not guarantee the solution will be implemented ethically or effectively. Further, sometimes these principles conflict with one another and point to different conclusions. For example, attending to the principle of compliance may help one to identify solutions that follow explicit standards of conduct. It will certainly help to keep one out of trouble with the law. But what about situations in which there are conflicting standards? Or no standards? In such situations, the principle of compliance can provide only limited information to guide ethical decision making.

As another example, the principle of consensus helps people avoid violating others' expectations within their society. But where exactly is the dividing line that separates those within and outside one's society? Also, what is the optimal percentage of people that need to agree in order to know that a true consensus has been obtained? If we consider the US as an example, there are vast differences in opinions about the ethicality of certain actions depending on one's political or religious affiliation. To make matters more complex, social consensus around issues can change over time. Thus, a decision considered ethical by individuals from one generation may be deemed unethical by those in the next, and vice versa. Social norms can also shift such that regulations are out-of-step with majority opinion, leading to a conflict between the principles of compliance and consensus.

Adhering to the principle of consequences may seem like a sure bet for making an ethical decision because this principle focuses on the actual outcomes of decisions. However, this principle can be used to justify a range of decisions that violate other more basic principles (e.g., human rights) in the interest of the 'greater good.' Clearly, depending on who is 'running the numbers,' the principle of consequences can be misused.

Also, we are limited in our ability to accurately predict in advance the exact outcomes of a decision. Put simply, good intentions are not enough. Sometimes well-intentioned decisions backfire because they are bad ideas, or because they are poorly implemented.

In sum, ethical decision making can, in some circumstances, be quite challenging. The 3 C's provide useful principles for determining if a decision is ethical and how to ethically implement these decisions. However, none of these principles is perfect. The most useful strategy is to consider all three principles in conjunction with one another. Whether one is an individual contributor, supervisor, mid-level manager, or executive, ethical decision making is the art of navigating ethical problems in ways that comply with rules, honor societal expectations, and maximize benefits while minimizing harm to others.

Ethical culture

There are stark differences between organizations as to which of the 3 C's that managers choose to emphasize. These principles, in turn, represent key elements of the organization's culture that influence how employees make decisions on a day-to-day basis. For example, it should not be a surprise that organizations with *compliance cultures* primarily emphasize the principle of compliance (Tenbrunsel & Smith-Crowe, 2008). These organizations invest significant resources in compliance systems—such as legal experts, auditing programs, and compliance training—that emphasize the enforcement of policies and regulations. The ultimate objective of compliance cultures is to prevent illegal and unsafe behavior in order to minimize organizational liability in the event that employees break the rules.

This prototype of a compliance culture is not what we mean when we use the term *ethical culture* throughout this book. Compliance cultures get only part of the ethical culture equation right. In other words, compliance systems are a necessary but insufficient aspect of any ethical culture. We define ethical culture as an environment where employees at all organizational levels are actively engaged in ethical decision making. This includes not only consideration of the principle of compliance, but the principles of consensus and consequences as well. Such organizational cultures are marked by frequent, deep, and open dialogue within and across organizational levels about ethical issues, their implications for stakeholders, and action plans for effectively preventing and dealing with ethical issues (Kaptein, 2011).

How ethical decision making works

While the 3 C's help define what an ethical decision is, these principles do not explain the psychological processes by which individuals generate and implement ethical solutions. What exactly is going on in the head of a person who is facing a dilemma? Understanding these psychological processes is important because they shed light on the steps that organizations might take to improve ethical decision making.

Reason versus intuition

Historically, researchers who study ethical decision making have tended to fall into one of two camps—the reasonists or the intuitionists. The reasonists dominated the early empirical literature on ethical decision making, which stretched from the 1960s to the 1980s. According to reasonists, ethical decision making involves a sequence of mental steps in which an individual consciously reasons their way to ethical action (Kohlberg, 1971; Rest, 1989).

The most popular model of ethical decision making championed by the reasonists involves four mental steps: (i) awareness, (ii) intention, (iii) judgment, and (iv) behavior. For a person to arrive at an ethical decision, first they must recognize that there is an ethical issue. Second, they must be motivated to make an ethical decision. Third, they must analyze the situation to determine the appropriate course of action. Finally, they must act. Many ethics training programs continue to draw upon the reasonist model of ethical decision making, with objectives centered around improving employee ethical awareness, intentions, judgment, and behavior (Steele et al., 2016).

Beginning in the 1990s, however, some researchers, who we refer to as the intuitionists, began to note significant shortcomings in the reasonist model of ethical decision making. Specifically, they noted that the reasonist model assumes that ethical decision making is a purely rational, deliberate, and conscious process. This assumption conflicted with decades of research coming out of the field of behavioral economics showing that much of human decision making is automatic, occurring at a subconscious level (Tversky & Kahneman, 1974).

The intuitionists described ethical decision making not as a series of deliberate mental steps, but as an automatic process based on people's 'gut instincts,' or intuition, in response to situational cues (Haidt, 2001). The intuitionists argued that these emotional, automatic processes are the primary means by which ethical decision making occurs. In this context, intuition refers to the feeling of moral rightness or wrongness associated with a decision. Intuition is deeply rooted in societal values—the social norms reinforced in one's early environment and experiences (Schwartz, 2012). According to the intuitionists, conscious reasoning processes only come into play after the fact when a person is asked to justify why a particular decision was made (Sonenshein, 2007).

Intuition plus reason

Both the reasonists and the intuitionists make some valid points about how ethical decision making occurs. But neither perspective is wholly satisfactory. People are not logic machines carrying out preformulated sequences of decisions. Nor are they irrational animals who always act without thinking. In other words, both intuition and reason clearly have a role to play in explaining the processes that people use to arrive at and implement ethical decisions. In recent years, researchers have proposed a hybrid model to explain how these processes work together. The hybrid model probably comes closest to accurately representing the subconscious and conscious mental processes that people use to make and implement ethical decisions, based on the best available evidence at this time (Reynolds, 2006).

The gist of the hybrid model is as follows. Most instances of ethical decision making are intuitive moral responses to everyday situations where appropriate and inappropriate courses of action are obvious. For example, telling the truth is a universal social value that, if followed, will result in ethical action in many circumstances with virtually no thought required. However, people sometimes face highly complex situations where knowing what is ethical and knowing how to act on this information is far from obvious. In such situations, reasoning processes become critical. For example, when people are faced with complex dilemmas, those who devote extra time to objectively thinking through ethical solutions and planning the implementation of these solutions tend to make better decisions (Watts, Medeiros, McIntosh, & Mulhearn, 2020).

Reasoning processes also play a critical role outside of the context of any specific ethical dilemma by supporting ethical learning over time. Here ethical learning refers to the process by which a person's intuition, or typical automatic response, is revised to better facilitate ethical decision making across a range of situations. Example activities that engage reasoning processes for ethical learning include reflecting on past or hypothetical events, practicing the development of action plans, and rehearsing the implementation of these plans. Just as savvy managers set aside time after each project to analyze what went well, what went wrong, and how to improve, reflecting on past decisions facilitates ethical learning that supports future decision making (Thiel, Bagdasarov, Harkrider, Johnson, & Mumford, 2012). This deep kind of learning is a key goal of any robust ethics training program. Through reflection and practice, employees can exercise their 'moral muscle memory,' building up resources for more intuitive ethical action (Arce & Gentile, 2015).

In sum, many models of ethical decision making have been proposed over the years. Currently, most researchers in this area recognize that both intuition and reason have important roles to play in ethical decision making. Next, we discuss several important psychological and organizational factors that have been shown to help or inhibit these processes. The model presented in Figure 2.1 illustrates the relationships between psychological and organizational factors and the decision processes that support ethical action.

Psychological factors

Researchers have identified three major psychological factors that help people identify and carry out ethical decisions at work. These factors include: (i) knowledge, (ii) skills, and (iii) personality. Psychological factors are internal. It is important to note that although internal factors are assumed to reside within individuals, these elements can be influenced by organizational factors, as shown in Figure 2.1.

Ethical knowledge

Ethical knowledge refers to the awareness and understanding of regulations, policies, guidelines, procedures, and norms that serve as relevant standards of professional conduct in one's organization, industry, and

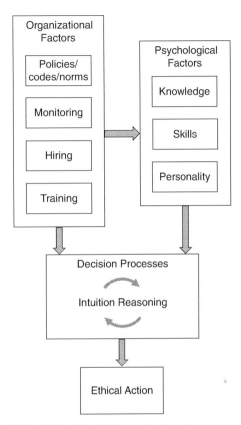

Figure 2.1 Model of Ethical Decision Making in Organizations.

profession. This knowledge can facilitate ethical decision making in two ways. First, knowledge of ethical standards can provide guidance concerning what decisions are defensible versus inappropriate or illegal, as well as guidelines for implementation. This guidance can simplify what might otherwise appear to be a complex dilemma, making ethical action more likely to occur. Second, when a person has knowledge of relevant ethical standards and procedures, they are less likely to break the rules out of ignorance. In other words, when a person is aware of ethical standards and procedures, they are less susceptible to violating these standards unintentionally.

Ethical skills

Knowing what is 'right' does not always translate into doing right. Ethical skills can help on both fronts—supporting the identification of ethical solutions as well as their implementation. Ethical skills refer to capabilities that facilitate ethical decision making and can be developed with practice. Researchers have identified a number of ethical skills. Some examples include reflecting on personal values, motives, and biases; managing one's emotions; and analyzing the short-term and long-term consequences of potential actions on various groups (Mumford et al., 2008). Additionally, skills that directly support implementation planning appear critical to ethical decision making. Implementation planning involves mapping out the key steps, players, and resources needed to execute a solution (Mumford, Mecca, & Watts, 2015). Implementation planning is the key process by which ethical ideas are transformed into ethical action (Gentile, 2010).

Ethical personality

Personality is a term used to describe relatively stable patterns in people's motivations and behavior. Due to their assumed stability, personality traits are not the focus of this book. Nevertheless, research shows that personality helps to explain ethical decision making in organizations, so the topic deserves some mention here. The top personality trait known to date that supports ethical decision making is conscientiousness. People with conscientious personalities are motivated to pay attention to social norms and exercise self-control to act in line with these norms. In other words, conscientious individuals are extra-focused on following rules—whether stated or unstated—in order to conform to others' expectations. For example, research shows that conscientious students are less likely to cheat and plagiarize in school (Giluk & Postlethwaite, 2015). In addition, employees with conscientious personalities commit fewer deviant behaviors at work, such as theft, substance abuse, property damage, and violating organizational policies (Salgado, 2002).

It is also important to note personality traits that can interfere with ethical decision making. People with ethical personalities tend to show lower levels of traits like narcissism, Machiavellianism, and psychopathy. Researchers commonly refer to these three traits as the 'dark triad'

(O'Boyle, Forsyth, Banks, & McDaniel, 2012). Narcissism refers to an unrealistic or inflated sense of self. People with narcissistic personalities can become so consumed with thinking about their own needs and goals that they forget to consider the welfare of others, resulting in unethical decisions (Antes et al., 2007). Machiavellianism is the tendency to view others as 'pawns' that can be manipulated for personal gain, which has been shown to skew ethical judgment (Pan & Sparks, 2012). Finally, psychopathy is a personality trait marked by a lack of empathy for others. People higher in psychopathy tend to show higher rates of unethical and antisocial behavior (Stevens, Deuling, & Armenakis, 2012).

Organizational factors

Even if a person has the right mix of ethical knowledge, skills, and personality traits, this does not guarantee they will make the right decision in every situation. A poignant example of this point may be observed in the now-famous series of 'learning' experiments conducted by the social psychologist Stanley Milgram and his colleagues at Yale University in the 1960s. Milgram found that more than half of the people brought into the lab were willing to deliver seemingly fatal amounts of electric shock to a stranger in another room at the insistence of an authority figure (Milgram & Gudehus, 1978). This is a finding that has since been replicated by other researchers in more recent years (Burger, 2009). An important conclusion emerging from this work is that some situational factors have the potential to disrupt ethical decision making even among normal and well-meaning individuals.

Researchers have identified a number of factors within the organizational environment that influence employee ethics. Here, we focus on the positive factors that have been found to improve ethical decision making. As shown in Figure 2.1, these factors support ethical decision making by creating an organizational environment in which ethical employees flourish. Four organizational factors that tend to help ethical decision making include: (i) policies, codes, and norms that prescribe ethical standards; (ii) reporting systems that expose unethical conduct; (iii) hiring systems that emphasize bringing in ethical talent; and (iv) training and development systems that develop ethical knowledge and skills. When deployed systematically, these factors jointly promote the reinforcement of ethical norms throughout the organization, contributing to the development and sustainability of an ethical organizational culture.

Policies, codes, and norms

Policies and codes refer to explicit rules, regulations, and guidelines established by the organization, industry, or profession. Policies and codes are critical resources for supporting ethical decision making because they specify the standards by which everyone agrees to operate. For example, in Coca Cola's Code of Conduct (2016) employees are encouraged to: Act with integrity, be honest, follow the law, comply with the code, and be accountable. Such standards form the foundation of ethical knowledge in each organization. They represent the 'rule book' that employees agree to operate by when they join the organization. Not surprisingly, educating employees about policies and codes is a key focus of many ethics training programs (Torrence et al., 2017).

In an ideal world, policies and codes would be followed. Of course, we know this does not always occur, otherwise there would be no need for a book on ethics training! There are many reasons why policies and codes sometimes fall short. Perhaps most importantly, if organizational norms contradict policies and codes, employees will be more likely to follow the norms. Norms refer to shared beliefs about how things actually get done in one's organization, industry, or profession. For example, when managers fail to hold accountable the employees who violate codes, this sends a strong signal that these codes are nothing more than 'window dressing' (Ford & Richardson, 1994). In sum, ethical organizations clearly communicate ethical standards and focus on making sure their deeds live up to their words.

Monitoring systems

Monitoring systems refer to the formal resources available to employees for reporting instances of observed or suspected misconduct as well as internal auditing systems that track compliance with standards of corporate governance (Weaver, Treviño, & Cochran, 1999). Examples of reporting resources include internal escalation protocols, such as when an employee submits a report to their direct supervisor or a designated organizational representative (e.g., HR, compliance) who is then responsible for following up on reports of misconduct. Other popular resources include 'ethics hotlines,' or websites where employees can submit anonymous reports internally or through third-party contractors.

Monitoring systems are a fundamental component of any ethical organizational ecosystem. These systems can help mobilize employees throughout all organizational levels to participate as ethical contributors. However, simply making such systems available is insufficient (Morrison, 2014). Employees must be trained on how to use these systems, and they must feel they can use these systems without fear of retaliation. Employees who receive the 'silent treatment' following reports are unlikely to use these systems again, and they may choose to escalate their concerns externally (Watts & Buckley, 2017). Monitoring systems can also help organizations to detect and address ethical issues early, before they have a chance to snowball into damaging events.

Hiring systems

Hiring systems refer to the procedures used to recruit and select new employees. Traditionally, organizations that emphasize ethics in their hiring systems have done so by integrating information about the importance of ethical values in job advertisements and including ethics-related assessments as part of the selection process (Osburg, Yoganathan, Bartikowski, Liu, & Strack, 2020). By advertising ethical values in job advertisements, organizations signal the importance of ethics to prospective employees, creating a 'first impression' of the organization as an ethical environment. Such a strategy may help to attract prospective employees who hold similar values (Adams, Tashchian, & Shore, 2001).

When valid ethics-related assessments are integrated in the employee selection process (e.g., integrity tests), organizations are doing more than signaling the importance of ethics. They are using scores from these tests to make better decisions about which job prospects to hire. For example, applicants who perform well on ethics-related assessments tend to demonstrate higher levels of job performance and lower levels of counterproductive behaviors at work (Van Iddekinge, Roth, Raymark, & Odle-Dusseau, 2012). As ethics-related assessments become more sophisticated, such tests may become even more useful for providing hiring managers with insights about the ethical knowledge, skills, and personality traits of various job prospects.

Training and development systems

Training and development systems refer to the formal and informal resources available to employees for continued ethical development on the job. By ethical development, we mean the learning of new knowledge and skills that support ethical decision making. Compliance and ethics training programs often serve as the most visible examples of these systems in many firms. Formal training programs such as these contribute to ethical decision making in a number of important ways that will be discussed in Chapter 3.

Training and development systems do not begin and end with formal ethics training programs, however. For example, ethical development can also occur through the performance appraisal process, as well as informal learning opportunities through interactions on the job with supervisors, coworkers, and customers (Ardichvili & Jondle, 2009). Although not the focus of this book, other informal learning opportunities can include lunch-and-learns, manager check-ins, online learning communities, networking at professional conferences, and even discussions among coworkers around the proverbial water cooler.

Conclusion

In this chapter, we defined key terms and summarized research on ethical decision making. Based on this information, two important conclusions should be noted. First, ethical decision making in organizations can be both simple and complex. In the modern organization—complete with systems of surveillance and other accountability structures that monitor and punish unethical behavior and reinforce compliance—much of ethical action is regulated. In this environment, many of the decisions confronting employees are straightforward instances in which right versus wrong paths are known and implemented intuitively based on prior experience or a basic knowledge of organizational policies and procedures.

However, ethical decision making is not always this straightforward. As employees take on increasing levels of responsibility and become accountable to more stakeholders, they are exposed to increasingly complex situations. When facing complex dilemmas, intuition and a basic knowledge of the rules may be insufficient to arrive at an ethical decision. In such situations, the knowledge and skills developed in ethics training may be especially critical.

Of course, effective ethics training programs prepare employees to respond to all types of ethical situations—whether black-and-white or gray.

Second, it should be clear from this chapter that ethics training is not a silver bullet. No matter how well designed, ethics training programs will not eliminate all instances of unethical behavior in organizations. A number of factors—both psychological and organizational—affect how employees behave regardless of the effectiveness of any ethics training program. For example, ethics training is unlikely to do much good in organizational cultures where managers with 'dark-side' personality traits are the norm instead of the exception. Imagine how futile such an ethics training program might have been if introduced at Enron in the months preceding the company's demise.

Even if organizations do an excellent job of hiring employees with ethical personalities and developing ethical knowledge and skills, a robust system of organizational factors must be in place to support ethical decision making. Organizations that fail to hold employees accountable for violating policies, or that discourage the reporting of unethical behavior either explicitly or implicitly, are unlikely to keep their ethical talent for long. In other words, managers must think about ethical culture from a systematic perspective to facilitate real and lasting culture change.

On the bright side, when applied systematically, ethics training can be an effective tool for helping employees develop the knowledge and skills needed to generate and implement ethical solutions. Such programs can also be useful for signaling the importance of ethics to internal and external stakeholders. In the next chapter, we address the effectiveness of these strategies by summarizing the research on the benefits of ethics training.

References

Adams, J. S., Tashchian, A., & Shore, T. H. (2001). Codes of ethics as signals for ethical behavior. *Journal of Business Ethics*, 29, 199–211.

Antes, A. L., Brown, R. P., Murphy, S. T., Waples, E. P., Mumford, M. D., Connelly, S., & Devenport, L. D. (2007). Personality and ethical decision-making in research: The role of perceptions of self and others. *Journal of Empirical Research on Human Research Ethics*, 2, 15–34.

Arce, D. G., & Gentile, M. C. (2015). Giving voice to values as a leverage point in business ethics education. *Journal of Business Ethics*, 131, 535–542.

Ardichvili, A., & Jondle, D. (2009). Integrative literature review: Ethical business cultures: A literature review and implications for HRD. *Human Resource Development Review, 8,* 223–244.

Burger, J. M. (2009). Replicating Milgram: Would people still obey today? *American Psychologist, 64,* 1–11.

Coca Cola Company (2016). Code of business conduct: Acting with integrity around the globe. Retrieved on December 3, 2019 from https://www.coca-colacompany.com/content/dam/journey/us/en/private/fileassets/pdf/our-company/2016-COBC-US-Final.pdf.

DuBois, J. M. (2008). *Ethics in mental health research: Principles, guidance, and cases.* Oxford, UK: Oxford University Press.

Ford, R. C., & Richardson, W. D. (1994). Ethical decision making: A review of the empirical literature. *Journal of Business Ethics, 13,* 205–221.

Forsyth, D. R. (1980). A taxonomy of ethical ideologies. *Journal of Personality and Social Psychology, 39,* 175–184.

Gentile, M. C. (2010). *Giving voice to values: How to speak your mind when you know what's right.* New Haven, CT: Yale University Press.

Giluk, T. L., & Postlethwaite, B. E. (2015). Big Five personality and academic dishonesty: A meta-analytic review. *Personality and Individual Differences, 72,* 59–67.

Haidt, J. (2001). The emotional dog and its rational tail: A social intuitionist approach to moral judgment. *Psychological Review, 108,* 814–834.

Kaptein, M. (2011). Understanding unethical behavior by unraveling ethical culture. *Human Relations, 64,* 843–869.

Kohlberg, L. (1971). Stages of moral development. *Moral Education, 1,* 23–92.

Lewis, P. V. (1985). Defining 'business ethics': Like nailing jello to a wall. *Journal of Business Ethics, 4,* 377–383.

Milgram, S., & Gudehus, C. (1978). *Obedience to authority.* New York, NY: Harper & Row.

Morrison, E. W. (2014). Employee voice and silence. *Annual Review of Organizational Psychology and Organizational Behavior, 1,* 173–197.

Mumford, M. D., Connelly, S., Brown, R. P., Murphy, S. T., Hill, J. H., Antes, A. L., Waples, E. P., & Devenport, L. D. (2008). A sensemaking approach to ethics training for scientists: Preliminary evidence of training effectiveness. *Ethics & Behavior, 18,* 315–339.

Mumford, M. D., Mecca, J. T., & Watts, L. L. (2015). Planning processes: Relevant cognitive operations. In M. D. Mumford & M. R. Frese (Eds.), *The psychology of* planning in organizations: Research and applications (pp. 9–30). New York, NY: Routledge.

O'Boyle, E. H., Jr., Forsyth, D. R., Banks, G. C., & McDaniel, M. A. (2012). A meta-analysis of the Dark Triad and work behavior: A social exchange perspective. *Journal of Applied Psychology, 97*, 557–579.

Osburg, V. S., Yoganathan, V., Bartikowski, B., Liu, H., & Strack, M. (2020). *Effects of ethical certification and ethical eWoM on talent attraction. Journal of Business Ethics, 164*, 535–548.

Pan, Y., & Sparks, J. R. (2012). Predictors, consequence, and measurement of ethical judgments: Review and meta-analysis. *Journal of Business Research, 65*, 84–91.

Rest, J. R. (1989). *Development in judging moral issues.* Minneapolis, MN: University of Minnesota Press.

Reynolds, S. J. (2006). A neurocognitive model of the ethical decision-making process: Implications for study and practice. *Journal of Applied Psychology, 91*, 737–748.

Salgado, J. F. (2002). The big five personality dimensions and counterproductive behaviors. *International Journal of Selection and Assessment, 10*, 117–125.

Schwartz, S. H. (2012). *An overview of the Schwartz theory of basic values. Online Readings in Psychology and Culture.* doi:10.9707/2307-0919.1116.

Sonenshein, S. (2007). The role of construction, intuition, and justification in responding to ethical issues at work: The sensemaking-intuition model. *Academy of Management Review, 32*, 1022–1040.

Steele, L. M., Mulhearn, T. J., Medeiros, K. E., Watts, L. L., Connelly, S., & Mumford, M. D. (2016). How do we know what works? A review and critique of current practices in ethics training evaluation. *Accountability in Research, 23*, 319–350.

Stevens, G. W., Deuling, J. K., & Armenakis, A. A. (2012). Successful psychopaths: Are they unethical decision-makers and why? *Journal of Business Ethics, 105*, 139–149.

Tenbrunsel, A., & Smith-Crowe, K. (2008). Ethical decision making: Where we've been and where we're going. *Academy of Management Annals, 2*, 545–607.

Thiel, C. E., Bagdasarov, Z., Harkrider, L., Johnson, J. F., & Mumford, M. D. (2012). Leader ethical decision-making in organizations: Strategies for sensemaking. *Journal of Business Ethics, 107*, 49–64.

Torrence, B. S., Watts, L. L., Mulhearn, T. J., Turner, M. R., Todd, E. M., Mumford, M. D., & Connelly, S. (2017). Curricular approaches in ethics education: Reflecting on more and less effective practices in instructional content. *Accountability in Research, 24*, 269–296.

Tversky, A., & Kahneman, D. (1974). Judgment under uncertainty: Heuristics and biases. *Science, 185*, 1124–1131.

Van Iddekinge, C. H., Roth, P. L., Raymark, P. H., & Odle-Dusseau, H. N. (2012). The criterion-related validity of integrity tests: An updated meta-analysis. *Journal of Applied Psychology, 97*, 499–530.

Watts, L. L., & Buckley, M. R. (2017). A dual-processing model of moral whistleblowing in organizations. *Journal of Business Ethics, 146*, 669–683.

Watts, L. L., Medeiros, K. E., McIntosh, T. J., & Mulhearn, T. J. (2020). *Decision biases in the context of ethics: Initial scale development and validation. Personality & Individual Differences.* doi:10.1016/j.paid.2019.109609.

Weaver, G. R., Treviño, L. K., & Cochran, P. L. (1999). Corporate ethics programs as control systems: Influences of executive commitment and environmental factors. *Academy of Management Journal, 42*, 41–57.

3

BENEFITS OF EFFECTIVE ETHICS TRAINING

Logan L. Watts

***

Anyone can claim that their ethics training program is effective. But is it really? How do they know? At a minimum, some managers may consider an ethics training program effective if all the employees who are required to complete the training have done so. Savvy managers, however, will want to know if their programs are having some real effect on the organization, such as how employees think, feel, and most importantly, act. In the following pages, we describe the procedures that researchers use to determine if an ethics training program is effective. For ethics training managers, understanding the procedures used to evaluate training effectiveness is critical. Finally, we highlight the benefits that managers can expect from investing in effective programs.

What is effective ethics training?

To understand what makes an ethics training program effective, it is first important to acknowledge that such programs come in many shapes and sizes. Ethics training is a label that gets applied to a variety of courses and programs (Mulhearn et al., 2017).

Here we draw on the Awareness-Analysis-Action framework to differentiate three major approaches to ethics training (Gentile, 2012). For example, some programs simply focus on raising ethical *awareness* by having trainees memorize rules and procedures. Others are aimed at improving ethical *analysis* to help trainees rationally weigh their options when facing a complex dilemma. Still others emphasize ethical *action* by having trainees plan and rehearse the implementation of ethical solutions.

Table 3.1 shows a comparison of how these three training approaches differ with respect to their foci, learning objectives, underlying assumptions, and activities. Clearly, there are many ways of 'doing' ethics training. At this point, however, we draw a distinction between what we refer to as *ethics training* and the traditional focus in organizations on *compliance training*.

Table 3.1 Major Approaches to Compliance and Ethics Training

General Focus	Compliance Training Awareness	Ethics Training Analysis	Action
Example learning objective	Increase knowledge of standards and procedures	Sharpen ethical thinking skills	Build 'moral muscle memory'
Underlying assumption	Poor decisions result from the ignorance or misunderstanding of expectations	Poor decisions result from immaturity, impulsivity, or inattentiveness	Poor decisions result from a lack of 'follow-through' on one's values
Example training activities	Listening to lectures on ethical issues; reading material on policies, procedures, and professional guidelines	Analyzing ethical dilemmas; writing essays; reflecting on biases; participating in discussions and debates	Developing action plans; writing and rehearsing scripts; practicing implementation via role-playing

Compliance versus ethics training

The primary goal of compliance training is to help employees learn the organizational rules and regulations that must be followed in order to mitigate liability and risk. Not surprisingly, compliance training tends to be designed by legal and policy experts who know these rules and regulations very well. The logic underlying compliance training in organizations is as follows. If employees have been educated about the rules, then the organization should not be liable if an employee decides to break the rules (Ferrell, LeClair, & Ferrell, 1998). Although this logic has some merit, it doesn't always hold up in court. For example, if organizations set up incentive systems that inadvertently encourage rule-breaking, the fact that compliance training was offered will not absolve the organization of liability. The 2016 Wells Fargo scandal provides a case in point (see Chapter 1). Although compliance training on its own can be useful for helping employees become more aware of the policies and regulations that apply in their organization, industry, or profession, such training on its own is insufficient for supporting ethical decision making.

In contrast, we use the label *ethics training* for programs that, broadly speaking, focus on enhancing ethical decision making. Chapter 2 described ethical decision making as a process consisting of two key components—*identifying* and *implementing* ethical solutions. Put simply, ethical decision making is about 'knowing good' and 'doing good.' However, not all ethics training programs place an equal emphasis on the *knowing* and *doing*. In fact, historically, ethics training programs have placed far greater emphasis on developing analytical skills that support the first component while assuming the second component—ethical action—will automatically follow (Gentile, 2013). This distinction between knowing and doing is reflected in the analysis and action approaches to ethics training presented in Table 3.1.

In distinguishing these approaches to ethics and compliance training, it might be natural to assume that programs always fit neatly into one of these categories. Often this is true in practice, but not always. Some programs manage to strike a balance between multiple foci. One such example can be observed in the professional ethics training program for early-career professionals at the University of Oklahoma (McIntosh, Higgs, Mumford, Connelly, & DuBois, 2018). In this two-day program, the predominant focus is on improving ethical analysis through case-based learning. However, ethical awareness and action also receive some attention, as demonstrated in the emphasis on learning professional guidelines, implementation planning, and role-plays. With this overview of different approaches to ethics training in mind, we now return to the question that started this chapter: How can we know if an ethics training program is effective?

Effectiveness

Broadly speaking, effective ethics training programs are those that demonstrate empirical success that their objectives are being met. There are two noteworthy components to this definition. First, there are many different types of compliance and ethics training programs with varying objectives. Differences in objectives may stem from differences in organizational standards, populations, industries, or geographic settings.

For example, educational institutions often require or encourage their students to participate in training programs focused on the promotion of academic integrity (e.g., citing sources properly, not cheating). In contrast, manufacturing firms may focus their ethics training programs on communicating safety or environmental standards mandated by the industry. Meanwhile, government agencies may be particularly concerned with educating employees about laws pertaining to bribery and the corruption of public officials. Finally, organizations operating in different local, state, federal, or international settings (see Chapter 12) can be subject to different standards and norms.

The second important feature of this definition of effective ethics training is the emphasis on empirical success. By *empirical*, we mean that there is objective evidence (i.e., data) suggesting that the program is meeting its objectives. However, not all forms of evidence are equally useful. Data may be collected from a variety of sources, using a variety of methods, to assess program effectiveness. These decisions about sources and methods have important implications that determine how strong the evidence is for a program's effectiveness (see Chapter 6).

Researchers have published many studies of ethics training courses and programs over the years. These studies have been conducted in academic, industrial, and government settings all over the world. In many of these studies, researchers collected and analyzed data in order to understand the effectiveness of the training. To do this, they estimated an effect size—a number used to understand how effective a training program is. Once an effect size can be estimated for a program, it becomes possible to compare and rank programs based on their effectiveness as well as identify the characteristics that make programs more or less effective. In other words, understanding effect sizes is a critical tool in the toolbox of any ethics training manager.

What is an effect size?

Readers are probably already familiar with a range of basic effect sizes used in everyday life. For example, one of the most common types of effect sizes is the percentage, in which scores on some variable are standardized using a 100-point scale. If one individual scores a 20% on a multiple-choice test, we can safely assume that this person answered most of the problems on the test incorrectly, even without knowing anything about the particular content of the test. Similarly, if a student scores an 'A' on their exam, we infer that this is a good score, regardless of the student's instructor, class, field, or institution. If a baby scores in the 90th percentile for head circumference, we know that the individual has a large head relative to other babies of their age. These are all examples of standardized measures used to help people make sense of data across a wide range of situations.

Because ethics training courses and programs use a variety of data sources and methods to estimate effectiveness, it is difficult to compare the results of these courses to one another in a meaningful way. These difficulties are solved by the effect size. The benefit of using effect sizes is that they allow for standardization of results across courses and programs. When effect sizes are available for many ethics training courses, we can use these standardized estimates to determine how effective a particular program is relative to other programs.

Perhaps more important, we can use effect sizes to make informed predictions about how effective a program is likely to be under different conditions. For example, if we find that ethics courses delivered via in-person or hybrid formats tend to have larger effect sizes than those delivered in a solely online format [which happens to be true; see Todd et al. (2017)], we might decide to invest in hybrid and in-person formats for future training efforts. However, if the goal of the course is to provide a brief refresher training on minor changes to industry standards, such a course might be more effectively communicated using online methods. Thus, we are not suggesting that managers ought to blindly implement whatever training techniques provide the largest effect sizes. Rather, effect sizes provide a valuable piece of information that, when weighed in the context of a program's goals and an organization's constraints, can be used to guide the design of effective ethics training programs.

Cohen's d effect size

When it comes to standardizing data from ethics training programs, the most common type of effect size used is Cohen's delta (sometimes written as Cohen's d or Δ), named after the statistician who developed the formula. Delta (Δ) is the Greek letter commonly used in mathematical formulas to denote change. In other words, Cohen's d is a formula used to estimate the size of the change, or difference, between two sets of scores. For ethics training data, the two sets of scores can refer to pre-training scores and post-training scores on some test. Or, the two sets of scores can refer to post-training scores for the training group and post-training scores for another group that did not receive the training (such as a control group).

Cohen's d works by converting the change, or difference, between two sets of scores into standardized units called standard deviations. These standard deviation units can then be used to estimate the effectiveness of ethics training programs and to compare programs to one another. A larger Cohen's d suggests that there is a larger difference between two sets of scores. There is technically no limit to the size of Cohen's d estimates, but researchers typically find values that range between -3.0 and $+3.0$ in most contexts, with a '0' indicating there is no difference.

Cohen (1992) offered the following guidelines for interpreting the size of the d metric. A Cohen's d of approximately $\pm.20$ represents a small effect, $\pm.50$ represents a moderate effect, and $\pm.80$ or above represents a large effect. Notice that Cohen's d can be negative or positive depending on the direction of the change in scores. See the Appendix at the end of this book for more information about how to calculate Cohen's d as well as additional online resources.

Benefits of effective ethics training

Some popular ethics training objectives that cut across organizational boundaries include improving knowledge and skills that support ethical decision making, contributing to an ethical organizational culture to help prevent misconduct, and reducing organizational liability when misconduct occurs. In this section, we summarize the scientific literature on the benefits that have been demonstrated by effective ethics training programs with respect to these three objectives.

Improved trainee knowledge, skills, and decision making

Many empirical studies have been conducted over the last several decades that investigate if ethics training courses or programs improve knowledge and skills that support ethical decision making. Here we will describe the findings of two meta-analyses. Put simply, a meta-analysis is a study of studies. A meta-analysis involves searching the scientific literature on a topic and then aggregating the results across all of the studies identified with the goal of identifying the 'true' relationship between two or more variables. In this case, the relationship we are most interested in learning about is the one between ethics training programs and trainee outcomes like knowledge, skills, and decision making.

The first meta-analysis we will describe focused on the results of ethics training studies conducted in the field of business (Medeiros et al., 2017). To be included in this meta-analysis, each study had to provide enough data to calculate a Cohen's d effect size. In total, the research team identified 46 ethics training studies that fit these criteria. These studies featured courses targeting a wide range of business-related populations and industries, including undergraduate business students, MBA students, and professionals in accounting, banking/finance, information technology, management, communication, and sales. Overall, the meta-analysis found that the 46 ethics training courses resulted in an average Cohen's d of .30. In other words, on average, ethics training programs in business appeared to benefit trainees to a small to moderate extent. However, the size of these benefits ranged considerably from one course to the next.

Along these lines, the researchers drilled down into the data to identify the features of particular programs that were associated with the greatest trainee benefits. The researchers found that ethics training programs were most effective when they targeted improvements in ethical decision making ($d = 1.16$), ethical behavior ($d = .58$), and moral reasoning skills ($d = .37$). In contrast, the programs targeting trainee attitudes ($d = .15$) and judgment ($d = .18$) tended to be less effective. In other words, ethics training programs were more successful when they focused on improving actionable skills rather than attitudes or feelings about particular ethical issues.

A second meta-analysis focused on ethics training programs in scientific fields—such as medicine, engineering, physics, chemistry, biology, and psychology (Watts et al., 2017). In total, 66 ethics training studies were included in this meta-analysis. The researchers found that, on average, ethics training courses yielded a Cohen's d of .48—a moderately large, positive effect.

Upon further analysis, these researchers found once again that ethics training courses varied considerably in their effectiveness depending on what they intended to achieve. Courses focused on improving trainee knowledge ($d = .78$), ethical decision making ($d = .51$), and moral reasoning skills ($d = .39$) were more effective than those attempting to improve trainee judgment ($d = .25$), conceptual abilities ($d = .24$), or trainees' general attitudes toward others ($d = -.01$).

When we consider the findings of these two meta-analyses together, a relatively clear picture emerges (see Figure 3.1). Across business and scientific fields, ethics training programs are more effective when they focus on improving trainee knowledge and skills that directly support ethical decision making. On the other hand, programs tend to be less effective when they focus on changing trainee perceptions of ethical issues, improving conceptual abilities that are rooted in stable cognitive traits (e.g., intelligence), or changing general attitudes about others. Clearly, ethics training programs can be highly effective when they are focused on achieving realistic objectives.

Stronger ethical culture

In Chapter 1, we summarized some of the benefits associated with an ethical organizational culture. Of course, effective ethics training can contribute to a stronger ethical culture by improving knowledge and skills

Figure 3.1 Average Cohen's d associated with ethics training outcome.

that help employees identify and implement ethical decisions. However, ethics training can also support ethical culture change by signaling to employees and other stakeholders (e.g., shareholders, customers) that ethics is a priority in the organization. In fact, whether meaning to or not, managers are continuously sending signals to employees about the behaviors that are valued in their organization based on where they choose to invest their limited resources and attention (Grojean, Resick, Dickson, & Smith, 2004).

Only a handful of survey studies have directly examined the relationship between ethics training programs and ethical culture. For example, Valentine and Fleischman (2008) surveyed a random sample of 313 managers from a wide variety of organizations and industries. They found that managers working in organizations offering formal ethics training programs reported stronger perceptions that their organizations were socially responsible, compared with managers working in organizations without such programs.

Additional evidence of the link between ethics training programs and ethical culture can be found in a study by Warren, Gaspar, and Laufer (2014). In this longitudinal study, employees at a large bank in the USA were surveyed immediately before, 9 months after, and 2 and a half years after the introduction of the bank's first company-wide ethics and compliance training program. The training program lasted approximately 4 hours. The content of the program focused on the company's values as well as compliance with policies and regulations. Key delivery methods for the program included engaging employees in case exercises that involved identifying and discussing instances of misconduct. Approximately half of the 2,200 employees in the company responded to one or more of the surveys. Nine months after the training, researchers found that:

- The number of observations of unethical behavior by employees decreased.
- The number of unethical behaviors that employees would be willing to report increased.
- The number of employees who would be willing to report unethical behavior increased.
- Employees' confidence in the organization's ability to appropriately handle instances of misconduct increased.
- Employees agreed more with one another about what constituted appropriate behavior.
- Employees perceived that the company's values were more important to both coworkers and senior managers.

In other words, effective ethics training programs not only increase knowledge and skills that support ethical decision making; they also change perceptions about the organization's priorities. These perceptions form the basis for a strong ethical culture.

Reduced organizational liability

An effective ethics training program can also be used to directly mitigate organizational liability in cases of criminal misconduct. When organizations or their employees engage in illegal activities, the organization and its directors may be held responsible for these offenses. The consequences for such offenses can include hefty fines and prison time, among others. For example, in the infamous case of accounting fraud at Enron, two chief executives received criminal convictions. While one of these executives died prior to sentencing, the other served 12 years in federal prison and was barred from serving as the financial director of companies in the future. Additionally, banks who participated in covering up Enron's fraud agreed to pay billions of dollars in fines to victims (Steele & Mumford, 2016).

The United States Federal Sentencing Guidelines were established in the 1980s and have been updated on a number of occasions, to inform sentencing penalties in cases of serious organizational misconduct. According to the guidelines, having an effective compliance and ethics program in place can help to reduce penalties faced by organizations in criminal cases (US Sentencing Commission, 2018). These guidelines define an effective compliance and ethics program as one in which the organization '[exercises] due diligence to prevent and detect criminal conduct' and 'otherwise [promotes] an organizational culture that encourages ethical conduct and a commitment to compliance with the law.' The guidelines specify seven minimum requirements that must be fulfilled for such a program to be considered effective, including:

- Developing organizational 'standards and procedures to prevent and detect criminal conduct'
- Installing a high-ranking organizational member or members as chiefly responsible for the program's effectiveness
- Excluding individuals with histories of criminal activity from organizational positions with 'substantial authority'
- Communicating periodically about standards and procedures by 'conducting effective training programs' (emphasis ours)
- Establishing monitoring and auditing mechanisms to help detect criminal misconduct, periodically evaluating program effectiveness, and providing and publicizing anonymous and confidential systems for reporting misconduct
- Reinforcing ethical standards and procedures through the consistent application of appropriate incentives and disciplinary measures
- Responding to instances of misconduct appropriately and updating procedures as necessary

The guidelines explicitly mention the importance of instituting periodic, practical, and effective ethics training programs. Of course, even robust and carefully designed programs will not eliminate all instances of misconduct, nor do such programs guarantee a 'get out of jail free card.' Nevertheless, training programs make a real difference as one piece of supporting evidence that the organization has taken reasonable steps to prevent misconduct, and as a result, such programs increase the likelihood of reduced penalties. Thus, by reducing potential organizational liability in instances of misconduct, effective ethics training programs have a direct impact on the organization's bottom line.

Conclusion

It is important to note a few limitations of some of the research discussed in this chapter. Most notably, we relied on studies published in the scientific literature to provide evidence for many of our arguments concerning the effectiveness of ethics training. A common issue that researchers face when evaluating empirical evidence is the file-drawer problem. The file-drawer problem refers to the tendency for statistically significant results to get published while papers with null results languish in 'file drawers' (Rosenthal, 1979). Because of the file-drawer problem, studies of unsuccessful ethics training programs likely have greater hurdles to overcome to get published. Put differently, it is difficult to find published studies of ineffective ethics training programs. As a result, the research referenced in this chapter may have over-estimated the benefits that can be attributed to typical ethics training programs.

With this limitation in mind, the research reviewed here points to a number of important conclusions. Although compliance and ethics training programs often differ in their objectives, along with other important features, clearly these programs can be effective in organizations and are worth the investment. In particular, ethics training programs can improve employee decision making, contribute to an ethical organizational culture, and limit organizational liability in the event of misconduct. But what are the specific features that separate the highly effective programs from the mediocre? In the following chapters, we address this practical question directly.

References

Cohen, J. (1992). A power primer. *Psychological Bulletin, 112,* 155–159.

Ferrell, O. C., LeClair, D. T., & Ferrell, L. (1998). The federal sentencing guidelines for organizations: A framework for ethical compliance. *Journal of Business Ethics, 17,* 353–363.

Gentile, M. C. (2012). Values-driven leadership development: Where we have been and where we could go. *Organization Management Journal, 9,* 188–196.

Gentile, M. (2013). Giving voice to values in the workplace: A practical approach to building moral competence. In L. Sekerka (Ed.), *Ethics training in action: An examination of issues, techniques, and development* (pp. 167–182). Charlotte, NC: Information Age Publishing.

Grojean, M. W., Resick, C. J., Dickson, M. W., & Smith, D. B. (2004). Leaders, values, and organizational climate: Examining leadership strategies for establishing an organizational climate regarding ethics. *Journal of Business Ethics, 55,* 223–241.

McIntosh, T., Higgs, C., Mumford, M., Connelly, S., & DuBois, J. (2018). Continuous evaluation in ethics education: A case study. *Science and Engineering Ethics, 24,* 727–754.

Medeiros, K. E., Watts, L. L., Mulhearn, T. J., Steele, L. M., Connelly, S., & Mumford, M. D. (2017). What is working, what is not, and what we need to know: A meta-analytic review of business ethics instruction. *Journal of Academic Ethics, 15,* 245–275.

Mulhearn, T. J., Steele, L. M., Watts, L. L., Medeiros, K. E., Mumford, M. D., & Connelly, S. (2017). Review of instructional approaches in ethics education. *Science and Engineering Ethics, 23,* 883–912.

Rosenthal, R. (1979). The file drawer problem and tolerance for null results. *Psychological Bulletin, 86,* 638–641.

Steele, L. M., & Mumford, M. D. (2016). Enron scandal. In S. G. Rogelberg (Ed.), *Encyclopedia of industrial and organizational psychology* (2nd ed.). Thousand Oaks, CA: Sage.

Todd, E. M., Watts, L. L., Mulhearn, T. J., Torrence, B. S., Turner, M. R., Connelly, S., & Mumford, M. D. (2017). A meta-analytic comparison of face-to-face and online delivery in ethics instruction: The case for a hybrid approach. *Science and Engineering Ethics, 23,* 1719–1754.

US Sentencing Commission (2018). *Chapter 8: Sentencing of organizations.* Retrieved on July 22, 2019   from https://www.ussc.gov/guidelines/2018-guidelines-manual/2018-chapter-8.

Valentine, S., & Fleischman, G. (2008). Ethics programs, perceived corporate social responsibility and job satisfaction. *Journal of Business Ethics, 77,* 159–172.

Warren, D. E., Gaspar, J. P., & Laufer, W. S. (2014). Is formal ethics training merely cosmetic? A study of ethics training and ethical organizational culture. *Business Ethics Quarterly, 24,* 85–117.

Watts, L. L., Medeiros, K. E., Mulhearn, T. J., Steele, L. M., Connelly, S., & Mumford, M. D. (2017). Are ethics training programs improving? A meta-analytic review of past and present ethics instruction in the sciences. *Ethics & Behavior, 27,* 351–384.

PART II

BEST PRACTICES IN ETHICS TRAINING IMPLEMENTATION

4

A MODEL OF ETHICS TRAINING IMPACT

Tyler J. Mulhearn

***

Start with the end in mind. This maxim applies to a variety of domains in life. Graduating from college, running a marathon, raising a child—each of these frequently sought-after achievements starts with an ambitious goal. When setting out to achieve a major life milestone, we often have grand visions of what the destination and journey might look like. A deep sense of satisfaction and meaning is often attached to the achievement of important goals—receiving the diploma, crossing the finish line, or watching a well-adjusted child transition into adulthood. Although major life milestones begin with a predetermined goal, a good amount of blood, sweat, and tears is often required to achieve that goal. In other words, a series of deliberate actions over an extended period of time is essential to reach such major milestones.

As with life milestones, ethics training milestones also start with an ambitious goal and require time and deliberate action over extended periods of time to achieve that goal. Starting with an end goal in mind and planning the steps to reach that goal are the foundation of any successful ethics training program. A C-Suite executive may admirably set out to improve the 'ethics' of the organization. This leader may communicate this vision to his or her directives and request a training program be developed to support this goal. What does improving 'ethics' mean and how does that occur? The responsibility of answering these questions and seeing the outcomes of these questions unfold in an organizational setting ultimately falls on the shoulders of ethics training managers. In particular, ethics training managers are responsible for developing, implementing, and monitoring ethics training programs. As a result, these managers play a key role in improving organizational ethics.

Exploring the series of decisions associated with developing a high-impact ethics training program is the primary focus of this chapter. More directly, this chapter offers a general overview of developing a new ethics training program by providing an overarching model of ethics training impact. It is our hope that this model will provide guidance to managers who are responsible for developing or administering ethics training programs in organizations.

Outcomes of effective ethics training

Regardless of the goals of an ethics training program, an ethics training manager typically aims to see some sort of improvement in the outcome of interest (Bell, Tannenbaum, Ford, Noe, & Kraiger, 2017). Given that the goal of any training program is to improve the skills, knowledge, or attitudes of trainees, the question then becomes: *What is the training program aiming to improve?*

Multiple objectives may be articulated for a training program. For example, an organization may set out to improve the ethical decision-making skills of employees or knowledge about the company's code of conduct. Alternatively, an organization may seek to improve the attitudes toward ethics in the workplace to foster a more ethical organization. Because ethics is a wide-ranging topic with multiple perspectives and disciplines ranging from philosophical values to pragmatic decision making (Mulhearn et al., 2017), an ethics training manager must determine the intended outcomes of the program prior to developing specific training content, evaluation measures, or materials for the training program. Similar to major life milestones, all subsequent decisions for developing ethics training programs are impacted by the initial establishment of an end goal.

How to know if ethics training has an impact

Assessing whether a goal has been achieved can be fairly straightforward in many cases. In the examples provided above, receiving a diploma, completing the marathon, and watching a well-adjusted child transition into adulthood are all reasonably objective outcomes. In the case of ethics training, determining its 'success' or overall impact is a much more challenging endeavor. To say that an ethics training program is 'effective' generally requires that data support this claim (see Chapter 3). To establish an impactful ethics training program requires an extensive amount of planning, content development, and evaluation.

To assess the impact of ethics training, two key decisions need to be made. First, evaluation measures, also known as assessments, must be selected or developed (Phillips, 2012). As discussed earlier, evaluation measures may include assessments of skills, knowledge, or attitudes in relation to ethics (Kraiger, Ford, & Salas, 1993). Second, the evaluation design must be determined to assess whether a change occurred as a result of the training program (Sackett & Mullen, 1993). A common example in this case is a pre-post training assessment of trainee knowledge about organizational policies. In the case of a pre-post assessment, trainees are asked to complete the same measure prior to and after training to see if the training program had an effect on the outcome of interest. Assessing the same outcome before and after training allows managers to see if the expected change in knowledge, skills, or attitudes actually occurred. The determination of whether a change in knowledge, skills, or attitudes occurred can be assessed by calculating an effect size (see Chapter 3).

Under the right conditions (see Chapter 9), ethics training can have wide-ranging effects on the decisions made by employees—decisions that by extension affect the daily operations of the organization as a whole. Over time, improvements in ethical decision making will be noticed by stakeholders, such as customers, suppliers, and the general public, resulting in a more positive perception of the organization. In sum, ethics training can have pervasive and long-lasting effects when conducted appropriately and supported at all levels of the organization (Campbell, 2007; Flammer, 2013).

The preceding discussion aimed to provide a general overview of evaluation as it relates to determining the impact of ethics training programs. For more detailed information on how to evaluate an ethics training program, see Chapter 6.

Model of ethics training impact

Up to this point in this chapter, we have devoted the majority of attention to training impact, or the extent to which an ethics training program achieves its intended outcomes. The emphasis placed on training impact is not accidental given its central role in understanding a broader systems approach to training. A systems approach to training involves an intentional effort to improve learning by specifying learning objectives, developing or selecting appropriate measures or criteria, and developing content and delivery methods aimed at achieving the established learning objectives (Goldstein & Ford, 2002). In short, a systems approach involves extensive planning.

A systems approach offers multiple benefits in designing and evaluating training programs. First, a systems approach allows the ethics training manager to consider the training system as a whole rather than a single component in isolation. As the name suggests, a systems approach views a training program as a system with interrelated components that all need to work together. To draw an analogy, the training program may be viewed as a machine in which the various pieces of machinery must operate in a synergistic fashion. If one piece of machinery is malfunctioning, the whole machine shuts down. Similar to the machine, every component of a training program must operate effectively, or else the whole system breaks down. An inexperienced trainer, unreliable outcome measure, or irrelevant training content can all drag down an otherwise impactful training program.

Second, a systems approach emphasizes the importance of feedback loops and opportunities for improving training. Feedback loops involve a cyclical approach to improvement where past experiences 'feed back' into future training development efforts. To draw another analogy, young children continuously experiment with the world around them to learn and adapt. Many parents encourage this behavior in their children to ensure they learn right from wrong and more and less effective methods of interacting with the world around them. Eventually, after trying numerous times, the child learns his or her own best way to walk, ride a bike, or catch a baseball. Just like the experimental young child, a training program requires continual refinement and improvement. The training program may require refinement based on trainee feedback, external regulations, or changing organizational standards and expectations.

Third, a systems approach reinforces the importance of learning objectives to ensure trainees acquire the knowledge, skills, or attitudes of interest in training. Learning objectives are clear statements of what trainees should be able to do as a result of the training program. Simply put, for trainees to understand what is expected of them, ethics training managers and trainers must first know what is to be achieved as a result of the training program.

Finally, as discussed in Chapter 3, novice ethics training managers may be tempted to select the various training characteristics, whether it be training content, delivery methods, or evaluation methods, that have historically been demonstrated to bolster training impact. This is a tempting yet risky approach to training considering that isolated training characteristics may not fit together in a cohesive fashion. Adopting a mentality of this nature would be similar to picking a single ingredient from each of your favorite meals and combining them all into one ultimate meal for the ages. What could possibly go wrong?! As anyone with any cooking experience would know, ingredients must complement one another to achieve a truly masterful dish.

Given the importance and high return on investment of a systems approach to training, we developed a Model of Ethics Training Impact to provide a framework for understanding how the various training features fit together to produce an impactful ethics training program. This model is supported by best practices recommended by ethics training research for delivering and implementing impactful ethics training programs.

More specifically, the Model of Ethics Training Impact presented in this chapter is adapted from another model tested by Watts et al. (2017). These researchers conducted a review of 235 ethics training courses and found this model explained 85% of the variance in ethics training effectiveness—that is, the effect size observed in the evaluation data collected for each course (see Chapter 3 for more information on effect sizes). In other words, this model received a substantial amount of empirical support. The Model of Ethics Training Impact described here provides a more straightforward visual representation of how the various training components relate to training effectiveness (see Figure 4.1). The Model of Ethics Training Impact is comprised of six components: training effectiveness, evaluation methods, content, delivery methods, planning, and transfer climate. Each component will be described in more detail below.

Training effectiveness

Training effectiveness refers to the extent to which changes in employee knowledge, skills, or other characteristics specified in training objectives are reflected in the evaluation data. In other words, measuring training effectiveness is the primary means by which we know if training had an impact. Given the close relationship between training impact and effectiveness, sometimes these words are used interchangeably throughout this book. All other training components presented in the model have been shown to influence estimates of training effectiveness in prior research.

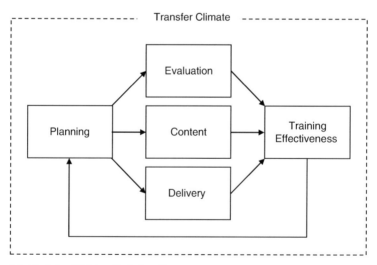

Figure 4.1 Model of Ethics Training Impact.

Thus, by attending to these key components, managers can increase the overall impact of ethics training. Training impact is inherently intertwined with the learning objectives established at the outset of training. These learning objectives establish what a trainee should learn or be capable of demonstrating by the end of training.

Evaluation methods

The assessment of whether or not learning objectives have been met by the training program is determined by the evaluation methods selected. Some evaluation methods are better suited than others for measuring the knowledge, skills, or attitudes that managers hope to change in ethics training. As a result, evaluation methods have a direct impact on statistical estimates of training effectiveness (see Chapter 6). Evaluation methods are indicators or markers of what the training program's learning objectives aim to achieve. For example, a training program with the learning objective of improving ethical decision-making skills of employees should administer an evaluation measure assessing ethical decision-making skills. If trainees generally show an increase in ethical decision-making skills on the evaluation measure following training in comparison to prior to training, this is an indication of training impact.

Content

To achieve the established learning objectives, an ethics training manager must develop and deliver content related to the learning objectives. Training content (see Chapter 7) may vary from educating trainees on organizational policies to privacy and confidentiality to strategies for improving ethical decision making. To use one of the examples provided above, an ethics training program may have the learning objective of improving ethical decision-making skills. The ethical training manager, then, might identify and determine ways to improve ethical decision-making skills that can be included in the training. This may involve the identification of appropriate strategies for improving decision-making skills or reducing potential biases that may harm decision making (DuBois, Dueker, Anderson, & Campbell, 2008; Watts, Medeiros, McIntosh, &

Mulhearn, 2020). Regardless, the content should be developed in line with the learning objectives.

Delivery methods

In turn, the delivery methods (see Chapter 8) selected for the training program should complement the training content to be delivered. In other words, the delivery methods should match the intent and focus of training content. Certain types of training content lend themselves better to passive learning techniques such as lecture, while others lend themselves better to active learning techniques such as role play or action planning. However, it should be noted that active learning techniques generally lead to better training outcomes by allowing trainees to engage with the material (Salas, Tannenbaum, Kraiger, & Smith-Jentsch, 2012).

The three training components discussed above—evaluation methods, content, and delivery methods—all play a key role in increasing, or decreasing, training impact. The systematic approach to developing each of these three training components can increase the impact of the training program. Deficiency in any of these three training components can lead to a less impactful training program overall. As a systems approach to training would suggest, a mismatch between these training components may also lead to reduced training impact.

Planning

The importance of ensuring evaluation methods, content, and delivery methods correspond with each other reinforces the importance of planning for ethics training (see Chapter 5). Planning, with a focus on the end goal, can facilitate the development of a more impactful ethics training program. Failure to plan may result in haphazard selection of evaluation methods, content, or delivery methods based on what is readily available or recommended by a senior manager or colleague. Although it may be tempting to select a quick and convenient approach, taking the necessary steps to plan and think through how the ethics training program elements fit together can go a long way in enhancing training impact.

Feedback loop

Once a training program has been implemented and evaluated, the next step is to learn from the insights obtained about the training program's effectiveness by feeding this information back into the planning component of the model. Training programs are never truly finished products (see Chapter 11), as one can use the information obtained from training evaluations to refine and improve the training program (McIntosh, Higgs, Mumford, Connelly, & DuBois, 2018). Often, this information is obtained by using evaluation methods to collect numerical data and trainee reactions at the end of training (i.e., summative evaluation) or throughout training (i.e., formative evaluation). See Chapter 6 for additional information on evaluation.

Transfer climate

Beyond the five key components of the Model of Ethics Training Impact, each element of the model is also influenced by the transfer climate (see Chapter 9). The transfer climate is the extent to which the work environment is supportive of trainees 'transferring' knowledge or skills learned in training to their jobs (Baldwin & Ford, 1988). As depicted in the model, transfer climate impacts all stages of the training design and implementation process.

Employees enter training with preconceived notions of what to expect based on prior training experiences, company policies, discussions with colleagues, and support (or lack of support) from leaders. These perceptions will, in turn, influence the level of motivation trainees have for learning while in the training program. Following training, the transfer climate can impact the extent to which trainees apply what they learned in training.

Conclusion

Managing ethics training programs involves a series of difficult decisions involving multiple stakeholder groups. Each decision can influence the overall impact of the ethics training program as well as broader outcomes for the organization and its stakeholders. Similar to running a marathon, graduating from college, or raising a child, a series of logical predetermined steps need to occur before reaching the end goal or learning objective. The

Model of Ethics Training Impact provides a means to organize the primary components of an ethics training program. Although this model is based on recent research, alternative versions of the model may be imagined. In this case, the model is intended to provide the reader with a useful organizing framework for ethics training. Now that a general framework for ethics training impact has been established, the next chapter will discuss the steps needed to plan out an impactful ethics training program.

References

Baldwin, T. T., & Ford, J. K. (1988). Transfer of training: A review and directions for future research. *Personnel Psychology, 41,* 63–105.

Bell, B. S., Tannenbaum, S. I., Ford, J. K., Noe, R. A., & Kraiger, K. (2017). 100 years of training and development research: What we know and where we should go. *Journal of Applied Psychology, 102,* 305–323.

Campbell, J. L. (2007). Why would corporations behave in socially responsible ways? An institutional theory of corporate social responsibility. *Academy of Management Review, 32,* 946–967.

DuBois, J. M., Dueker, M. J. M., Anderson, E. E., & Campbell, J. (2008). The development and assessment of an NIH-funded research ethics training program. *Academic Medicine, 83,* 596–603.

Flammer, C. (2013). Corporate social responsibility and shareholder reaction: The environmental awareness of investors. *Academy of Management Journal, 56,* 758–781.

Goldstein, I. L., & Ford, J. K. (2002). *Training in organizations* (4th ed.). Belmont, CA: Wadsworth Cengage Learning.

Kraiger, K., Ford, J. K., & Salas, E. (1993). Application of cognitive, skill-based, and affective theories of learning outcomes to new methods of training evaluation. *Journal of Applied Psychology, 78,* 311–328.

McIntosh, T., Higgs, C., Mumford, M., Connelly, S., & DuBois, J. (2018). Continuous evaluation in ethics education: A case study. *Science and Engineering Ethics, 24,* 727–754.

Mulhearn, T. J., Steele, L. M., Watts, L. L., Medeiros, K. E., Mumford, M. D., & Connelly, S. (2017). Review of instructional approaches in ethics education. *Science and Engineering Ethics, 23,* 883–912.

Phillips, J. J. (2012). *Handbook of training evaluation and measurement methods.* London: Routledge.

Sackett, P. R., & Mullen, E. J. (1993). Beyond formal experimental design: Towards an expanded view of the training evaluation process. *Personnel Psychology, 46,* 613–627.

Salas, E., Tannenbaum, S. I., Kraiger, K., & Smith-Jentsch, K. A. (2012). The science of training and development in organizations: What matters in practice. *Psychological Science in the Public Interest, 13,* 74–101.

Watts, L. L., Medeiros, K. E., McIntosh, T. J., & Mulhearn, T. J. (2020). *Decision biases in the context of ethics: Initial scale development and validation. Personality & Individual Differences.* doi: 10.1016/j.paid.2019.109609.

Watts, L. L., Mulhearn, T. J., Medeiros, K. E., Steele, L. M., Connelly, S., & Mumford, M. D. (2017). Modeling the instructional effectiveness of responsible conduct of research education: A meta-analytic path-analysis. *Ethics & Behavior, 27,* 632–650.

5

PLANNING FOR TRAINING IMPACT

Tristan J. McIntosh

***

Imagine that you have been asked to prepare a delicious meal for a group of friends. Where would you begin? You might ask your friends if there are any particular foods they especially like or dislike. After all, you wouldn't want to spend hours preparing the meal to find out that two of your friends are allergic to the ingredients you used. Before going to the grocery store, you would likely want to decide on a recipe and write down a list of needed ingredients. Showing up to the grocery store unprepared would likely result in not getting the right type or amount of ingredients for the recipe you will be preparing.

Much like the considerations needed for planning a dinner party, implementing an ethics training program requires planning and forethought. In this chapter, we discuss practical first steps ethics training managers can take to increase the likelihood of developing an impactful ethics training program. This includes how to conduct and leverage organizational and environmental analyses, garner support from relevant organizational stakeholders, and identify gaps in employee competencies needed for ethical decision making and ethical action. All three of these planning elements combine to inform the development of an ethics training program.

Organizational analysis

Before devoting the time, money, and effort to develop an ethics training program, it is essential for managers to determine how prepared the organization is to implement such training. An organizational analysis is a broad, system-wide assessment that helps managers to evaluate an organization's readiness for change. Ethics training programs have a higher likelihood of achieving their objectives when these programs align with the organization's strategic goals, are supported by employees at all levels, have access to necessary resources, and address relevant ethics competencies. In sum, those seeking to develop and implement an ethics training program should first identify the factors that are likely to influence the effectiveness of the ethics training program prior to planning training content and execution.

Strategic goals

Ideally, every organization values and strives toward an ethical workplace to some degree. This goal is often interwoven within the organization's business strategy. For example, Aflac, an American insurance company that has been publicly recognized for being one of the World's Most Ethical Companies for 13 consecutive years (Aflac, 2019), has established a strategic commitment to ethics. This strategic goal, in turn, guides how organizational leaders prioritize ethics, how customers are treated, and how the ethical culture is shaped, which includes ethics training. Those who wish to implement ethics training at their organization should first identify the organization's strategic goals and determine whether or not that business strategy includes tenets of an ethical workplace (Noe, 2013).

If it does not seem that an organization's business strategy prioritizes ethics in the workplace, conversations must take place with those in the upper-management level. Those in upper management are often the ones to make decisions about what policies, practices, and initiatives are established within an organization. Demonstrating how ethics initiatives could give the organization a competitive advantage may convince those in upper management that investing in ethics training is worthwhile (see Chapter 1). For example, comparing the cost of a major ethics scandal to the anticipated cost of rolling out an ethics training program may lead those in upper management to realize its value. Upper managers may also view ethics initiatives more favorably if they are made aware that training programs can help contribute to a strong ethical culture, which is positively associated with various metrics of organizational success (see Chapter 1).

Organizations that incorporate ethics into their business strategy, on the other hand, are likely to allocate a greater amount of resources (e.g., money, personnel) to an ethics training program than organizations that prioritize ethics less (Combs, Liu, Hall, & Ketchen, 2006). Implementing larger-scale ethics initiatives, such as organization-wide ethics training, is a key way to demonstrate an organization's commitment to ethics. Given the span of large-scale ethics training initiatives, it is essential to have support from key decision makers within the organization (i.e., upper management) in order for these initiatives to be successful.

Support for training

It is not sufficient to only have support from upper management. Rather, support is also needed from those in middle management, supervisors, and individual contributors. Those in middle management should be willing to champion the ethics training to their employees, provide their employees with encouragement to take and pay attention to training, and provide guidance on applying the skills acquired during ethics training to their jobs (Rouiller & Goldstein, 2002). The messaging surrounding the new ethics training program will be essential. Do managers make the training sound engaging to their employees? Meaningful? Practically useful? An opportunity for professional development?

Similarly, individual contributors, or frontline employees, will benefit more when they have some degree of enthusiasm about the ethics training and motivation to actively participate in it. Managerial encouragement, making training content relevant to employees' jobs, and rewarding employees for taking the ethics training are likely to foster enthusiasm and motivation. If frontline employees and managers are unsupportive and unenthusiastic about the ethics training program, the training is unlikely to be successful. While support and enthusiasm are important for the success of a new ethics training program, there are other factors that can act as barriers to effective implementation.

Resources and roadblocks

Barriers to effectively developing and implementing the ethics training, along with essential resources, should be identified and considered well before any official training development or implementation takes place. One question to consider is whether there is resistance to mandating employees to take yet another training. If employees perceive the training to be a waste of time instead of an opportunity for development, they will not take the training seriously and any attempts at improving training effectiveness will be thwarted.

Other questions for consideration include whether the budget is available for designing an ethics training program from scratch and whether the organization has the expertise and resources needed to design and conduct an ethics training. Designing an ethics training program from scratch requires considerable time from multiple people within the organization, space to conduct the training, and the capacity to protect employee time for taking training. Given the unique complexities of ethical issues and skills required to design and implement an effective ethics training program, it is essential that organizations prioritize hiring personnel with the appropriate expertise to design and implement ethics training initiatives. It is unlikely that legal, policy, and compliance-focused expertise will be sufficient to improve ethical decision making beyond increasing awareness of rules and regulations. Expertise in the psychology of ethical decision making, as well as knowledge of the training and adult education literatures, are also critical. As will be discussed in Chapter 6, organizations will also need to have the capacity to test the effectiveness of their training, which could require multiple administrations of various assessments. If an organization is unable to develop, implement, and evaluate an ethics training program from scratch, seeking the assistance of external consultants with ethics training expertise is a viable alternative.

Another consideration is whether there is something in the work environment that could derail training effectiveness. If trainees do not have the opportunity to apply what they learned during training or are not rewarded for doing so, it is unlikely that any positive effects of training will be seen. If managers do not reinforce concepts taught during training and do not encourage employees to share with others what was learned during training, it is unlikely to have a meaningful impact. Providing trainees with the resources to apply what they have learned during training, such as access to decision-making tools or a reporting hotline, will increase the likelihood that they apply what was learned during training to their jobs. Along related lines, if the organization does not show that it values, at a broad level, what is taught in the ethics training, it is highly unlikely that the ethics training will be successful at improving ethical decision making and 'moral muscle memory' on the part of employees (Gentile, 2012). More information will be provided in Chapter 9 about how to improve the post-training work environment to optimize ethics training impact.

Identifying key competencies

An organization's core competencies are skills or abilities that employees have which can help meet organizational goals, including ethics-related goals. These competencies are cross-cutting throughout the organization and are relevant to all employees, regardless of their position within an organization. Examples of ethics-related competencies include knowledge of industry standards and skills that facilitate ethical decision making and action (see Chapter 2). These competencies can help set an organization apart from its competitors. Assessing varying levels of ethics-related competencies within different units of an organization can signal whether particular groups of employees need more targeted ethics training attention. Chapter 7 provides detail on how developing competencies can be incorporated into ethics training content.

Environmental analysis

Understanding the broader ethical environment in which an organization is situated can help organizations identify ethical issues that are most likely to be faced by its employees. This process can be referred to as an environmental analysis. Information from an environmental analysis will be critical for developing and selecting ethics training content. Chapter 11 provides some guidance on monitoring the external environment for the purposes of ongoing program refinement, but the following sections will provide information about initial environmental analysis for developing ethics training content.

Analysis of regulations

Understanding, from a bird's-eye view, how an organization is positioned in the broader regulatory environment can help ethics training program managers identify what regulations are most pertinent to the organization's operations. Specifically, identifying and understanding relevant federal, state, regional, and industry-specific laws and regulations can establish what employees must know or do in their jobs when it comes to ethics and compliance. This information may differ depending on the group of employees within an organization. It may be that a certain subset of employees need to take an ethics training that covers particular topics, depending on the industry in which they work. For example, engineers need far more knowledge of manufacturing codes operating within their industry than accountants. Therefore, specific subsets of employees may need to take a more tailored ethics training compared to other employees that do not face these particular ethical issues.

Common versus unique ethical issues

Both common ethical issues and ethical issues unique to specific groups within an organization need to be identified and integrated into training. While certain ethical issues may be pertinent at all levels of an organization, different ethical issues may emerge as more important or frequent among different organizational units and teams. Developing a sense of the types of ethical issues that employees face at various positions within an organization can help ethics training program managers identify content areas to be covered during ethics training. Identifying these issues can also serve the purpose of collecting original ethics case examples from experienced employees. Case examples are short scenarios or stories that illustrate key learning points. These case examples can then be used as activities that take place during training. Chapter 8 provides more detail about how cases can be used in ethics training.

To identify common ethical issues, ethics training managers can take a number of approaches. Surveys are an efficient way to reach a large number of employees, maintain anonymity and confidentiality of employee information and perspectives, and gather a representative sample of ethical issues. For example, electronic surveys can be administered to employees asking about the frequency and details of ethical issues they face. An alternate approach could be to conduct focus groups or interviews with employees, asking them to share ethical issues they have faced or ethics-related concerns. However, for this approach to work, trust and rapport must be built with employees so that they feel safe sharing their concerns and ethical issues without fear of reprimand. Table 5.1 presents types of questions that can be asked to employees when undertaking a variety of training impact planning activities, which help maximize the impact of training.

Table 5.1 Example Questions for Learning about Ethical Issues in Organizations

Training Impact Activity	Example Questions to Ask Employees
Identifying common ethical issues	• How frequently do you encounter ethical issues at work? • What are common types of ethical issues you face on your job? • Describe a time where you were faced with an ethical dilemma at work. • Within the last [week/month/quarter/year] how many times have you had to deal with [insert type of ethical issue]?
Obtaining employee perspectives	• What types of situations call for ethical action on your job? • What challenges do you encounter in relation to managing ethical issues on the job? • What aspects of your work environment make addressing ethical issues easier? • How important is ethical behavior to your boss? To organizational leadership? • When unethical behaviors are noticed, how quickly are they addressed? How effectively are they addressed?

Stakeholder buy-in

Buy-in, or commitment, from employees at all levels of the organization, including those in upper management, middle management, and frontline employees, will be essential for the training to come to fruition and be successful (Bennis, 1969). Communicating with these stakeholders and rounding up support for a new ethics training initiative will need to occur early in the planning process. This is a task that is often easier said than done. Below we provide several helpful hints for 'selling' a new ethics training program to all three stakeholder groups. Each group can have different objectives and be motivated by different factors, which is why a tailored approach for each group is needed.

Upper management

This stakeholder group is perhaps the most central to getting a new ethics training program off the ground. Those in upper management will be the ones who make the decision of whether or not to devote money, time, and energy to a new training program. Ethics training managers will need to communicate the vision of the envisioned ethics training. By providing upper managers with information about the type of data an organizational analysis will produce, expected outcomes of the ethics training, and how training outcomes will contribute to the organization's bottom line, they are more likely to see the value of an ethics training program.

A number of external awards and recognition programs designed to reward organizations that make ethics a priority exist (e.g., Ethisphere Institute). Making upper management aware of these programs, which can boost the reputation of the organization, may make the argument for implementing ethics training more compelling. Additionally, getting support from upper management is particularly important due to a trickle-down effect to middle managers and other employees (Noe, 2013). That is, securing upper-management buy-in upfront sets the tone that ethics should be a priority for middle managers and employees because it is a high priority for upper management.

Drawing the connection between a new ethics training program and other human resources (HR) practices (e.g., other training programs, se-lection, performance management, compensation) can provide upper

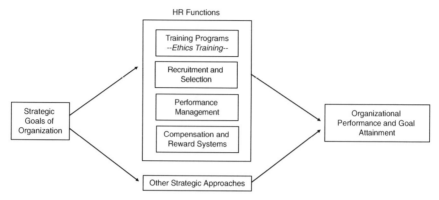

Figure 5.1 Ethics Training in the Context of HR Functions.

management with a big-picture view about how a new training would fit within the broader system. Figure 5.1 depicts how ethics training might fit with other HR practices.

The strategic goals of an organization affect how various HR functions and other strategic approaches are executed, which ultimately serves to influence organizational performance and goal attainment. Of the HR functions shown, ethics training falls under the Training Programs component of HR functions. Prioritizing ethics as a strategic goal would serve to influence all HR functions, such that there would be an ethical element to each. That is, ethics as a strategic goal would also inform recruitment and selection decisions, performance management decisions, and compensation decisions. This would then contribute to the achievement of ethics-related goals, such as reducing the number of ethical violations that occur within an organization.

In addition to demonstrating to upper management how ethics training fits in the broader context of HR functions, it is also important to manage expectations and to avoid over-promising. Ethics training managers should avoid telling upper management that the training is guaranteed to increase the firm's profitability, but they can provide data-informed estimates of a range of benefits—both financial and nonfinancial—that tend to be associated with a strong ethical culture (see Chapter 1). Demonstrating the value of the training program by providing estimates about the return on investment can be worthwhile (Flammer, 2015). Managers can also communicate with senior leaders about how an ethics training program can help reinforce ethical values throughout the organization. In sum, it is important to communicate why upper managers have a vested interest in seeing the ethics training become successful (Tannenbaum, 2002).

Middle management

While those in middle management may not have the same degree of resource-providing power for developing a new ethics training program as upper management, they will be essential for supporting the training while planning the training content and once training is in place. That is, they will be the ones to help advertise and champion the training to frontline employees by coordinating trainee schedules and ensuring that trainees are able to take time away from regular work tasks. Middle management will also be the ones to reinforce training concepts once trainees have completed the ethics training.

To demonstrate the value of a new ethics training program to those in middle management, ethics training managers will need to illustrate ways in which the ethics training will help departments be more effective in attaining departmental objectives. This could be accomplished, for example, by showing data on how ethical decision making is associated with higher levels of performance and customer satisfaction, or lower levels of counter-productive work behaviors. When communicating with upper management, ethics training program managers should focus on the impact that an ethics training program will have on organizational outcomes that upper management values. Communication should be straightforward and to the point about how an ethics training program will strategically help the organization's bottom line (Grant, 2015). By identifying what middle managers value and demonstrating how a new ethics training contributes to those values, middle management will be more likely to support such an initiative.

Frontline employees

Frontline employees encompass lower-level managers and supervisors, individual contributors, and entry-level employees. Convincing frontline employees that taking part in a training program is worth their attention, time, and motivation is essential. Buy-in from frontline employees can be influenced by how a new ethics training program is advertised, whether the training is perceived as job-relevant, and the degree to which employees are rewarded and encouraged to apply what they learned in training to their jobs. Visible support and enthusiasm from upper management, middle management, and frontline employees' supervisors about the training will signal to frontline employees that it is important and valued by the organization. For example, frontline employees may be motivated by the idea that ethical employees are more likely to be promoted within their organization. If those in management do not appear to value the training or take the training seriously, neither will other employees who are asked to take the training. When those in management communicate and act in ways that support the content covered in ethics training, employees in turn may feel more empowered to take action and to speak up before ethical issues arise (Gentile, 2012).

Another factor likely to increase employee buy-in is making training content engaging. If ethics training is perceived to be 'just like every other training' employees have previously taken, they are unlikely to take it seriously. Additionally, they may be likely to only go through the motions of attending training just to 'check the box.' Demonstrating how ethics training will help frontline employees do their jobs better and make them more successful in their roles will increase their motivation to attend and learn from training. Identifying benefits of ethics training that are both intrinsically and extrinsically meaningful to employees can motivate individual ethical action (Fudge & Schlacter, 1999). For example, managers can demonstrate that more ethical employees are likely to be promoted or provide periodic rewards or other forms of recognition to individuals or teams for structuring 'ethical action reviews' into meetings. If the work environment and organizational leaders are not supportive of using what was learned during training, then frontline employees are also unlikely to feel empowered to take ethical action. To create a supportive environment, trainees should have opportunities to practice what they learned during training and be encouraged and rewarded by organizational leaders for doing so appropriately.

In sum, all of the aforementioned stakeholder groups will need to be convinced that a new ethics training program is worth the resources, time, and energy needed for the program to be successful. However, how these stakeholder groups are approached and communicated with regarding the new ethics training program should be tailored to their values and goals. Support for developing and implementing a new ethics training program is an element of planning that should not be overlooked.

Employee readiness

Employee readiness is characterized by whether or not the employees in an organization are able and willing to take part in training and whether or not they possess the characteristics needed to learn from the training (Noe, 2013). It is something that should be accounted for when designing an ethics training program because of its impact on employee learning. If employees are not ready to take part in training, then the training will not be effective. In what follows, strategies for determining employee readiness are discussed.

Identifying trainees

An important consideration when planning for training impact is to determine which employees should take ethics training. Should it be all employees within the organization? Employees from a particular department or team? Employees who are in leadership positions? Or employees in frontline positions? While there is not a one-size-fits-all approach to ethics training in organizations, the greatest training effects are likely to be seen when the messaging provided during training is aligned throughout all levels of an organization (Warren, Gaspar, & Laufer, 2014). That is, if all employees receive some type of ethics training that communicates the same message, even if the specific content of that training differs slightly, then everyone will be on the 'same page.' This alignment reinforces cultural norms and expectations surrounding ethics at all levels within an organization which helps to maximize the impact of training.

For example, if an organization's stated values include professionalism, all trainings would communicate what professionalism is and how it should be upheld. However, specific training content for entry-level employees may focus more on professionalism in day-to-day interactions with customers, whereas training content for middle managers may focus more on professionalism in managing their employees or finding new clients for the organization. Training cases, discussions, and other activities may differ between groups of employees, but the value of professionalism will be woven throughout.

It may not be feasible or desirable to train all employees within an organization at once. Demonstrating training feasibility in one department or group of trainees can lend credibility to the training, paving the path for rolling out the ethics training at a larger scale within the organization. More information about how to design and implement a pilot training can be found in Chapter 10. Regardless of the approach taken, it will be important to identify the gaps in competencies, or ethics-related employee knowledge, skills, and abilities. Competencies should be aligned with the strategy and goals of the organization and set the organization apart from its competitors. Pinpointing competency gaps related to an ethical workplace allows for prioritization of who should receive training, when they should receive training, and where the content of training should be focused.

Competency gaps

Identifying competency gaps at the organizational level can provide insight as to what group of employees should take more targeted ethics training and the degree of readiness to take ethics training. However, it is valuable for organizations to offer ethics training to all employees, regardless of whether ethics competency gaps exist. At the outset of identifying competency gaps, it is important to answer the question of whether current or expected ethical performance on the part of employees indicates that more, and more targeted or remedial, ethics training is needed. Considerations include whether ethical transgressions have taken place within the organization and within various teams or departments, whether employees feel comfortable speaking up about ethical issues at work, if there have been changes to certain jobs or job families that warrant additional ethics training, and if there have been changes to organizational or field norms and policies that call for ethics training. This information can signal what group of employees might benefit most from further ethics training.

Obtaining employee perspectives

To further identify prospective trainees, actually hearing the perspectives of these individuals will provide additional unique information. This can be done through in-person interviews or focus groups or online questionnaires that employees complete. Table 5.1 provides examples of questions that can be asked to employees about their ethical experiences and struggles on the job. Asking questions of this nature also sheds light on whether or not ethics training is the best and only solution for reducing unethical behavior and cultivating ethical behavior. Perhaps there is an element in the work environment or a particular protocol that makes it difficult for employees to behave ethically. However, caution and proper judgment are warranted when dealing with confidential or sensitive information provided by employees. Establishing a psychologically safe environment for employees to share these issues will result in more candid, accurate, and useful information (Liu, Liao, & Wei, 2015).

Finally, asking employees about ethical issues they perceive in their work is critical, as they have the greatest knowledge about their jobs and the ethical issues typically faced on these jobs. They will be able to provide valuable input and insight that might not otherwise be considered when determining who needs ethics training and what type of content should be covered in this training. This information can signal what learning objectives should be established for the new ethics training program as well. Employee involvement in this phase of planning simultaneously acts as a mechanism for motivating them to take part in training and applies the training to their jobs. By taking the time to involve employees and obtain their input, they will be better able to identify, articulate, and plan for ways they can take action in response to ethical situations (Gentile, 2012). This valued perspective can provide insight as to what specifically can be done to make training content both meaningful, relevant, and actionable.

Conclusion

Planning for the implementation of an ethics training program is a significant undertaking requiring a substantial amount of time and effort. While it may seem daunting to obtain and sift through all of the information needed to effectively plan for training impact, this information only serves to strengthen the content of the ethics training program and maximize its effectiveness. Multiple iterations of information gathering and conversations with relevant organizational stakeholders may need to take place before and after getting approval for a new ethics training initiative.

Taking the time to plan for any new ethics training initiative is worth the effort and investment. Without an informed plan in place, ethics training managers will be 'flying blind' in creating a new ethics training program, which will likely result in a training program that falls below expectations. By using key information from an organizational analysis, obtaining support from all relevant stakeholders within an organization, and identifying who would benefit most from training, training managers will have an arsenal of information and support needed for an ethics training program to be effective.

References

Aflac. (2019, February). Aflac one of the world's most ethical companies for 13th consecutive year. *Press Release*. Retrieved from: https://investors.aflac.com/press-releases/press-release-details/2019/Aflac-One-of-the-Worlds-Most-Ethical-Companies-for-13th-Consecutive-Year/.

Bennis, W. (1969). *Organization development: Its nature, origins, and prospects.* Reading, MA: Addison-Wesley.

Combs, J., Liu, Y., Hall, A., & Ketchen, D. (2006). How much do high-performance work practices matter? A meta-analysis of their effects on organizational performance. *Personnel Psychology, 59*, 501–528.

Flammer, C. (2015). Does corporate social responsibility lead to superior financial performance? A regression discontinuity approach. *Management Science, 61*, 2549–2568.

Fudge, R. S., & Schlacter, J. L. (1999). Motivating employees to act ethically: An expectancy theory approach. *Journal of Business Ethics, 18*, 295–304.

Gentile, M. C. (2012). Values-driven leadership development: Where we have been and where we could go. *Organization Management Journal, 9*, 188–196.

Grant, A. (2015). Your guide to communicating with upper management. *Fast Company*. Retrieved on June 7, 2020, from: https://www.fastcompany.com/3049998/your-guide-to-communicating-with-upper-management.

Liu, S. M., Liao, J. Q., & Wei, H. (2015). Authentic leadership and whistle-blowing: Mediating roles of psychological safety and personal identification. *Journal of Business Ethics, 131*, 107–119.

Noe, R. A. (2013). *Employee training and development.* New York, NY: McGraw Hill.

Rouiller, J., & Goldstein, I. (2002). The relationship between organizational transfer climate and positive transfer of training. *Human Resource Development Quarterly, 4,* 377–390.

Tannenbaum, S. (2002). A strategic view of organizational training and learning. In K. Kraiger (Ed.), Creating, implementing, and managing effective training and development (pp. 10–52). San Francisco, CA: Jossey-Bass.

Warren, D. E., Gaspar, J. P., & Laufer, W. S. (2014). Is formal ethics training merely cosmetic? A study of ethics training and ethical organizational culture. *Business Ethics Quarterly, 24,* 85–117.

6

IDENTIFYING EVALUATION CRITERIA AND METHODS

Tristan J. McIntosh

***

Designing the evaluation process for an ethics training program is similar to purchasing a house. When purchasing a house, there are generally two options. Will you build a brand new house from scratch? Or will you buy an existing one? If you build a new house, a finished product will likely take more time and effort than buying an existing house, but you will have the opportunity to design it in a way that exactly suits your preferences, needs, and available resources. Newly built houses are also less likely to need repairs compared with older houses. If you buy an existing house, it may already have the basic features you need, but it will not be customized based on your particular preferences. The differences between purchasing an existing house and building a new house are analogous to the approaches that can be taken to evaluate an ethics training program.

Failure to properly evaluate ethics training programs can ultimately undermine training effectiveness and in some cases produce more harm than good (Antes & DuBois, 2014). If training is not having its intended effect, then it is likely wasting a great deal of organizational resources. This cost comes in the form of time, money, and process loss that is incurred with conducting an ineffective training program. Moreover, without evaluation to signal when a training is effective, employees might take away the wrong lessons during training that may lead them to act or think in ways not intended by training developers. Such unintended outcomes can negatively affect employee decision making.

Fortunately, there are straightforward steps that ethics training managers can take to effectively evaluate training and maximize training outcomes. The goal of this chapter is to provide a practical, evidence-based summary of why it is important to evaluate ethics training programs, how to evaluate these programs, and how to use this evaluation data strategically to benefit your organization.

Why evaluate training?

It is important to remember that not all ethics training programs are created equal. Why invest valuable and scarce resources in ethics training that fails to improve ethical action? After investing in ethics training, evaluating its effectiveness can provide a strong case for its return on investment. In other words, determining the impact of ethics training on trainees and the organizational context in which these individuals work demonstrates the training program's value (Goldstein & Ford, 2002). This is especially important when making a case to upper management about the need for designing and implementing a new ethics training program or overhauling existing programs that are dated or ineffective.

Unfortunately, many ethics training programs are never evaluated, and many of those that are evaluated are done so to 'check the box' using inadequate assessment practices (Steele et al., 2016). For example, a 2016 report by Deloitte and Compliance Week found that the measures used to assess compliance training effectiveness—such as training completion rates—are often inappropriate and provide little useful information about the training's actual effectiveness. Adopting a more systematic approach to training evaluation is worth the investment because organizations can use this information to continually optimize the program's impact on employee decision making and ethical action. In other words, training evaluation helps to support real, lasting culture change.

When training evaluation is approached haphazardly, programs may have no effect on employee decision making, or may unintentionally lead employees to disengage when confronted with ethical issues in the workplace. For example, if an ethics training includes extreme case examples of people engaging in unethical behavior, trainees may end up thinking that they would never engage in such extreme unethical behavior. This, in turn, can lead trainees to disengage from the idea that they might actually be susceptible to engaging in unethical behavior and think that the ethics training does not really apply to them (Antes et al., 2012). Alternately, exposing employees to too many of the nuances and complexities of ethical dilemmas may overwhelm or discourage them, resulting in the avoidance of work issues involving ethical considerations. Such disengaged attitudes can lay the groundwork for costly unethical behavior in the future (Watts, Medeiros, McIntosh, & Mulhearn, 2020). Conversely, an ethics training program may result in overconfidence in one's ability to address ethical issues in the workplace, making employees perceive that they are invincible to making unethical decisions. Both extremes can result in damaging consequences to unsuspecting individuals, teams, or the organization. Thus, training that incorporates a variety of realistic scenarios—including both complex and everyday dilemmas that allow trainees to practice acting on their values (Arce & Gentile, 2015)—may be particularly impactful (see Chapters 7 and 8). The point here is that managers should not automatically assume that ethics training is having a positive impact without investigating the data.

Failure to appropriately evaluate whether the objectives of an ethics training program have been met is problematic for several reasons. First, without evaluation, there is limited accountability for the outcomes of training. That is, without evaluation, there is limited information to measure the benefits of training relative to costs. Managers will need to justify the need for training resources to upper management, and training program evaluation provides insights to support these conversations. Second, without evaluation, it is difficult to pinpoint what training content or exercises contribute to desired or undesired outcomes. Finally, without evaluation, there are limited mechanisms for maintaining and improving training effectiveness over time. Evaluation data informs what training content and types of exercises should be included, who should receive training and when, and how to maintain lasting effects of training in the workplace after training has concluded.

How to evaluate training

Determine desired outcomes

The first step to evaluating a training program is to determine what the specific desired outcomes, or learning objectives, of training are. Do you want employees to be able to know and apply organizational policies related to ethics? Do you want to improve ethical decision-making skills? Do you want employees to feel empowered to take ethical action? Do you want employees to improve at recognizing when unethical behavior occurs? Do you want to create an organizational culture grounded in ethics? While not all training programs are likely to achieve every possible desired outcome, taking time to think through the purpose of the ethics training program will provide the foundation for informative program evaluation.

Thus, prior to making decisions about ethics training content, managers should identify the learning objectives of the training. Learning objectives are measurable (i.e., observable) outcomes that define what trainees are expected to be capable of doing after completing training. Learning objectives are comprised of three components: (i) the conditions when trainees are expected to perform the behavior, (ii) the behavior of trainees, and (iii) the outcome that signals how well the behavior was executed (Goldstein, 1980). Here are some example statements of learning objectives that might be used to guide the design of ethics training programs:

- Trainees will be able to identify common ethical issues that arise in the industry.
- Trainees will incorporate key ethical principles into their decisions when faced with an ethical dilemma.
- Trainees will understand the available resources and procedures for reporting ethical issues.
- Trainees will be able to initiate discussions about ethical concerns that emerge in their work with peers and managers.
- Trainees will develop a plan to take action when ethical issues emerge.

Types of training outcomes

There are four general types of training outcomes that can be used to evaluate training effectiveness: (i) trainee reactions, (ii) trainee learning,

(iii) trainee behavior change, and (iv) organization results (Kirkpatrick, 1996). Table 6.1 provides examples and brief descriptions of these four types of ethics training criteria. In discussing these four types, we are not suggesting that managers should only select one type of outcome to evaluate. In fact, it is generally recommended to collect multiple types of outcome data. Doing so provides a comprehensive view of how the ethics training is working and what elements should be changed to further improve training effectiveness (Mumford, Steele, & Watts, 2015).

Trainee reactions

It is essential that trainees perceive the training program to be valuable and relevant to them professionally. If trainees are satisfied with training content, training administration, and the trainers who conduct the training, they will likely be more motivated to learn and more likely to apply what they learned during training on the job. In a review of 381 ethics training sessions, it was found that favorable trainee reactions are strongly, positively correlated with trainee learning (Turner et al., 2018). Measuring the extent to which trainees think the training was engaging, informative, and relevant are all types of reactions measures that can be used to evaluate and improve the training program. For example, trainees can be asked, using a 1 (strongly disagree) to 5 (strongly agree) scale, to rate how much they liked the course, how relevant the course content was to their jobs, how satisfied they were with the training instructors, and how likely they would be to recommend the training to coworkers. In addition to obtaining these general reactions to the training, it can also be beneficial to ask trainees more specific questions about particular content or activities covered in training. Such data can provide managers with detailed insights for improving particular aspects of the ethics training.

Trainee learning

A common objective of ethics training is to help trainees learn the attitudes, knowledge, and skills that support ethical decision making in their work. It is critical to incorporate evaluation measures that allow managers to judge the extent to which desired learning objectives such as this have been met. For example, if the objective is for trainees to be capable of

Table 6.1 Examples of ethics training criteria

Ethics Training Criteria	Description	Examples
Reactions	Reactions measures assess trainee perceptions of an ethics training program, including the overall training and specific training modules. Reactions measures are typically administered at the conclusion of each training session.	• Motivation to apply training content • Satisfaction with training • Perceived relevance of training content to job • Satisfaction with the training instructor
Learning	Learning measures assess what trainees have learned as a function of taking ethics training. Learning can take the form of changes in attitudes, knowledge, and skills related to ethics in the workplace. These measures can be administered at the beginning and end of training to determine whether training had the intended effect. Or learning measures can be measured as a post-test only if trainees only need to meet a minimal standard of performance.	• Attitudes about the importance of ethics in the workplace • Ethical sensitivity • Knowledge of an organization's ethics policies • Knowledge of where to locate whistleblowing resources • Ethical decision-making skills • Values-driven communication skills
Behavior	Behavioral outcomes indicate whether and how trainees apply to their job what they learned during ethics training. Because of the amount of time it takes for trainee behaviors to change after taking ethics training, consideration should be given as to when gathering behavioral outcome data should occur.	• Number of reports of misconduct or unethical behavior • Use of whistleblowing resources • Number of whistleblowing reports • Instances of theft • Instances of counterproductive work behaviors • Peer observations of (un)ethical behavior

(Continued)

Table 6.1 (Continued)

Ethics Training Criteria	Description	Examples
		• Peer observations of speaking up to both other peers and managers • Self-report measures of (un)ethical behavior • Self-report measures of speaking up to both peers and managers • Measures of team psychological safety • Team reports of problem-solving approaches
Organizational results	Organizational results indicate the payoff of an ethics training program for the organization as a whole. These outcomes are influenced by multiple factors, so it may be challenging to determine the exact effect ethics training has on these outcomes.	• Ethical organizational, department, and team culture • Employee productivity • Number of industry awards for being an ethical organization

applying professional decision-making strategies to solve ethical problems, one could administer an assessment of professional decision-making skills (DuBois et al., 2016). In another example, if the objective is for trainees to understand the regulatory requirements applying in their field, then it is important to measure if knowledge about the details of relevant regulations has, indeed, improved following training. Further, if the goal is to develop 'moral muscle memory' (Gentile, 2012), evaluation measures might involve assessing competencies related to forming and implementing action plans, re-framing situations to highlight ethical elements, and identifying allies to help address ethical issues.

Trainee behavior

Following training, trainees should be able to apply what they learned and, ideally, behave differently in their day-to-day work. Many measures of behavior change are possible. Examples include the number of times reporting procedures or whistleblowing resources (e.g., hotline) are used and the frequency of informal communications with peers and leaders about ethical issues as they emerge. A popular approach to evaluating trainee behavior is through surveys. For example, trainees can be asked questions such as:

How prepared do you feel to deal with values conflicts?
What strategies and scripts do you utilize when navigating values conflicts?
How often do you have problem-solving-focused conversations about potential values conflicts with your manager and coworkers?

The number of counterproductive work behaviors (CWBs) can also be measured. CWBs, such as theft, sabotage, bullying, and harassment can harm organizational productivity and employee well-being (Spector & Fox, 2005). In fact, CWBs such as these have been shown to cost organizations billions of dollars annually (Bennett & Robinson, 2000). Ethics training can help with decreasing the occurrence of CWBs as well as increasing the use of ethical behaviors (see Chapters 3).

Organizational results

Because a number of factors determine whether ethics training results in tangible effects on organizational results, this is often the most challenging type of training outcome to assess. Examples of organizational results include increased employee productivity; job satisfaction and retention; improved perceptions of ethical culture; and even business unit profitability. Organizational reputation or industry awards related to ethics are other 're-sults' that might be realized over time as outcomes of effective ethics training initiatives (e.g., Ethisphere). The effects of ethics training on organization results can be difficult to detect, and they can take a considerable amount of time to be observed. Along related lines, factors outside the control of the organization, such as the economy or political climate, can have powerful effects on organizational outcomes. Although it is certainly challenging to quantify the effects of ethics training on broader organizational results, savvy managers can use a number of evaluation strategies discussed here to determine the long-term returns on investments in ethics training.

Select evaluation measures

Once learning objectives are identified, the next step involves selecting appropriate evaluation measures that will allow managers to assess the extent to which these objectives are realized. Different evaluation measures assess different outcomes. Choosing which evaluation measures to use is similar to a doctor selecting the right medical tools to diagnose a patient's health. For instance, a stethoscope can be used to learn about a patient's heart health, but would be inappropriate for evaluating the health of a patient's eardrum. Similarly, a measure of ethical decision-making skills can be used to assess if trainees have developed these skills and are able to apply them, but such a measure should not be used to evaluate trainees' knowledge of organizational policies and standards.

Selecting appropriate evaluation measures provides the foundation for judging the success of ethics training. The measures selected ultimately determine what conclusions can be drawn about the effects of training. Ethics training managers face a number of important decisions when selecting evaluation measures. One important decision involves whether to use a pre-made, off-the-shelf evaluation measure or develop a custom evaluation measure from scratch. If a new measure is desired, those who develop it should be experts to ensure best practices in test design and validation are followed (Boateng, Neilands, Frongillo, Melgar-Quinonez, & Young, 2018). Test development is a complex and labor-intensive process that involves defining the specific competencies to be evaluated, generating test content, and assessing reliability and validity. When carefully designed, custom measures that are tailored for the specific training population can deliver more precise information about ethics training effectiveness compared with off-the-shelf measures (Watts et al., 2017). However, given the additional time, resources, and expertise needed to develop new evaluation measures, training managers may opt to sacrifice some precision and use previously validated, off-the-shelf measures.

Before selecting an off-the-shelf evaluation measure, managers should gather as much information about the reliability and validity of the measure, as well as the types of populations where the measure has been used in the past. For example, test publishers should be asked to provide technical information about the number of people who have completed the measure as well as summary demographic information about these individuals (e.g., organizational size, type of field/occupation, industry, geographic region). Other questions that should be asked include:

> What evidence is available that this measure will deliver consistent results across different groups?
> Have experts established if the content of the measure represents the competency intended?
> What is the estimated amount of time needed to complete the measure and cost per use?
> Are there additional costs involved in scoring the measure? Are there alternative versions of the measure available that have been established as equivalent?

Such questions can help ethics training managers determine whether a certain measure is appropriate for evaluating their ethics training program.

Regardless of whether evaluation measures are developed from scratch or off-the-shelf, an adequate degree of reliability and validity is needed to be confident that these measures are accurate and of high quality. A reliable measure is one that is consistent in what it measures over time and across different groups of people. A valid measure is one that provides accurate information about whatever variable it claims to measure. Every measure falls somewhere on a continuum of validity, and where each measure falls on that continuum varies by the amount and strength of supporting evidence (Messick, 1995). For example, if you ask a person what his or her favorite color is, it is likely that the question, or measure, will elicit the same, reliable response when the question is asked a second time in the future. However, asking a person a favorite color is probably not a valid measure of critical thinking skills. Thus, it is critical that ethics training managers select reliable and valid evaluation measures that consistently and accurately reflect trainee differences on the desired training outcome.

As a variety of evaluation measures exist, so do a variety of test formats that vary in length and type of data collected. Different evaluation formats might be useful for assessing different outcomes. Many evaluation measures take the form of a Likert scale, which involves asking trainees to rate their responses to statements or questions using an interval scale (e.g., 1 to 5 scale). For example, a reactions measure may ask trainees to rate the relevance of a certain training module on a scale of 1 (not at all relevant) to 5 (highly relevant). Likert scales are also useful for measuring other kinds of ethics-related outcomes frequently captured in surveys (e.g., behavioral self-reports, other-reports, attitudes).

Other evaluation formats take the form of multiple-choice, where trainees are asked to select the correct answer among a set of answers. This format is frequently used to assess trainee knowledge, but it can also be useful for evaluating ethical judgment. Situational judgment tests present trainees with brief, realistic vignettes that pose an ethical dilemma. Trainees are then asked to identify what action they would take in response to the vignette among a set of answer options (Clevenger, Pereira, Wiechmann, Schmitt, & Harvey, 2001). This test format has also proven useful for assessing decision-making skills and cognitive processes related to ethical decision making (Mumford et al., 2006; Mumford et al., 2008).

Another useful evaluation format is obtaining qualitative data from trainees using interviews, focus groups, or open-ended survey questions. Qualitative data can provide rich information that numeric measures do not. Qualitative measures can be used to assess the effectiveness of training, as well as learn about the specific aspects of training that trainees found most or least useful and why. As a result, qualitative measures are an important tool to incorporate in ethics training evaluation efforts (Watts et al., 2017). In sum, all of these evaluation formats have unique strengths that, when used appropriately, can provide valuable information to ethics training managers.

It may be tempting to administer only one evaluation measure, such as a reactions measure, to evaluate an ethics training program because it is quick and easy to administer. However, program evaluation is based on a pattern of findings, and there is no silver bullet of ethics training evaluation. Therefore, ethics training managers should use multiple measures to evaluate different outcomes, so long as these measures are tied to learning objectives. Using a variety of measures provides the greatest amount of evidence for the effectiveness of an ethics training program. Moreover, using multiple evaluation measures enables ethics training managers to better identify which aspects of training are deficient or are particularly effective. Demonstrating evidence of program effectiveness also helps to justify current and future investments in the ethics training program.

Select evaluation design

Once the desired outcomes of training have been determined and the appropriate evaluation measures have been selected, it is also necessary to determine the evaluation design. Evaluation can take place either after training (i.e., post-test) or both before and after training (i.e., pre-test, post-test). Pre-test evaluation can be used to compare trainee performance to a predetermined benchmark. Pre-test evaluation can also provide ethics training managers with a baseline of trainee performance. This baseline enables comparisons of pre-training performance and post-training performance on a given measure. Post-test evaluations can take place in the absence of pre-testing or in tandem with pre-testing. Post-test-only approaches to evaluation are typically used when the purpose of the ethics training is to demonstrate that trainees have reached a minimum level of mastery or competence. Post-testing accompanied by pre-testing can be used to determine whether the training improves performance, and it also enables the size of this effect to be calculated (Cohen, 1992). Post-testing can occur at multiple time points after training to determine whether the effects of training are long lasting or if there is a short peak in performance immediately following training with a decline in performance over time. Effect sizes can be used to determine the magnitude of training effects over time.

Another mechanism that can be used to evaluate the effects of training is to compare the outcomes of a training group to a control group. Assuming that all employees will eventually take part in ethics training, staggering the timing of when certain groups actually take part in training can help create viable control comparison groups. A control group would take the same pre-test and post-test as the training group, but would not participate in training in between testing. The control group would take the training at a later point in time. Randomization should be used to decide which employees or units should be in the control group versus the initial training groups.

Finally, subject matter experts can also be used to establish benchmarks to determine if trainees have demonstrated satisfactory progress on particular outcomes (Ricker, 2006). Scores below a certain threshold, informed by subject matter experts, could indicate that trainees did not learn what they needed to learn; scores at or above a certain threshold could indicate trainees did learn about regulatory requirements during training.

Strategies for implementing evaluation

At first, it may seem daunting to decide what evaluation measures should be administered and when. Many considerations must be taken into account. However, with some careful thought and planning, evaluation can be skillfully and strategically timed to provide the most useful data to ethics training program administrators. Table 6.2 provides a list of practical questions that ethics training managers should answer as they implement evaluation measures.

Among these practical considerations are determining the mode and timing of distribution, which are decisions that should be made when planning ethics training program evaluation.

Will assessments be distributed electronically using survey software?
Will they be administered in person using paper and pencil?
Will pre-training assessments be taken before the scheduled training or on the first day that trainees arrive to training?
At what point will post-training assessments be taken? Immediately after training? A week after training? A year after training?

Evaluating the short-term and long-term effects of ethics training can be useful to assess the staying power of intended outcomes.

Additional consideration is warranted with implementing and interpreting data from evaluation because ethics can be a sensitive topic for many employees. Because of this, the measurement of ethics-related outcomes may be affected. For example, self-report measures of ethical or unethical behavior may not be very useful for getting an accurate picture of these outcomes because respondents may try to answer questions in a manner that will be viewed favorably by others. However, there are strategies for improving the accuracy of behavioral reports on sensitive topics, such as promising employees anonymity in their responses and framing questions to ask about coworker behavior instead of personal behavior. In what follows, multiple strategies for implementing the various approaches to evaluation are discussed.

Table 6.2 Practical questions to consider when implementing training evaluation

Evaluation element	Questions
General evaluation questions	• Which evaluation measures align best with the learning objectives of your ethics training program? • Are your evaluation measures both reliable and valid? • Will you use off-the-shelf evaluation measures? Or will you develop your own? • Will you use field-specific or field-general evaluation measures? Or both? • At what frequency will you administer each evaluation measure? • What mode will you administer evaluation measures?
Reactions measures	• What information from trainees will be helpful to improve your ethics training program? • Are there reactions questions about the general, overall training? Are there reactions questions about specific components of the training?
Learning measures	• Will the evaluation measures be administered at multiple time points? • How long will it take to see the effects of ethics training on learning outcomes?
Behavioral measures	• Are self-report behavioral measures subject to social desirability bias? • How long will it take to see the effects of ethics training on behavioral outcomes?
Organizational results	• What other non-training factors are influencing this outcome? • How long will it take to see the effects of ethics training on organizational outcomes?

Reactions

Reactions measures should be administered immediately at the conclusion of each day of training. This is because trainees will be able to quickly and easily recall what they did and did not like about training. The effects of training on reactions measures are very short term. Reaction-based assessments can also be administered to trainees prior to training as part of an organizational analysis, as discussed in Chapter 5. Pre-training reactions assessments provide a good opportunity to collect critical information needed to plan for and monitor ethics training program effectiveness, including trainee perceptions about the ethics training program and attitudes about ethics in the workplace more broadly.

Learning

Learning measures, such as those of attitudes, knowledge, and skills, can be administered both before and after training, depending on the purpose of the ethics training program. If the goal of evaluation is to assess long-term learning and retention of training material, these measures can be administered once, immediately after training and again after a specified period of time has lapsed. It is important to note that attitudes may take a longer amount of time to change compared to knowledge and skills. This is because attitudes are more subjective in nature and are rooted in personal values and beliefs, whereas skills and knowledge are more objective (Kraiger, Ford, & Salas, 1993). In addition to reactions measures, knowledge, skill, and attitudinal evaluation measures are most likely to be influenced by ethics trainings compared to the more distant, long-term behavioral and organization-level effects described below (Kirkpatrick, 1983).

Behavior

In most cases, it requires time and a multitude of other environmental factors for behavior change on the job to occur after training has been completed. Such required factors include trainees' motivation to change behavior, whether expectations for behavior change are set by managers, whether employees are praised or rewarded for the behavior, and whether institutional norms and policies support behavior change (Noe, 2013).

Instances when managers set sub-optimal ethical expectations for employees may derail employee ethical action and make it less likely that employees apply what they learned during ethics training to their jobs. However, ethics trainings may still help inoculate employees to some extent against negative managerial influence by equipping employees with strategies for speaking up and taking action.

Other behavioral outcomes of ethics training include, but are not limited to, the number and severity of ethics-related complaints linked to an employee, self-report measures of (un)ethical behavior, and peer observations and reports of wrongdoing. Because multiple factors influence (un)ethical behavior, ethics trainings may not always result in immediate, drastic changes in ethical behavior. However, immediate behavior change following ethics training is possible, but it may be due to unique reasons. For example, after completing ethics training, trainees' awareness about ethical issues is heightened, so trainees may be more likely to discuss ethical issues openly with their peers and speak up about ethical concerns, as well as identify and report ethical issues that they encounter on their jobs.

A decision will need to be made about whether all employees receive the same ethics training content or if there are certain modules or versions of training that a particular group of employees will take. When only a certain subset of employees take an ethics training, organization-wide ethical behavior change should not be expected. Moreover, employees at different levels or roles within an organization (e.g., mid-level manager, entry-level employee) may need to attend ethics trainings with different content that is more tailored to their job. For example, employees who work in different departments (e.g., accounting, marketing) are subject to different rules and regulations and may need to take different versions of ethics training that relate to relevant rules and regulations. Regardless of how many versions of an ethics training exist within an organization, the type of evaluation measures used should be tailored to and directly aligned with the content of each version of training.

However, some evaluation measures may be similarly applied to multiple employees (e.g., knowledge of an organization's policies, attitudes about ethics, perceptions of an ethical culture). For example, measures of ethical organizational climate are relevant to all employees, are broadly tied to employee ethical behavior, and can be used as a proxy for assessing ethical behavior in the workplace (Cullen, Victor, & Bronson, 1993).

While this relationship is complex, aspects of the work environment influence the ethical behavior of all employees. Assessing organizational climate in addition to the aforementioned behavioral outcomes provides a more comprehensive picture of the work environment and its effects on employee behavior.

Organizational results

To identify relevant organizational metrics, ethics training program managers can seek both archival data sources and newly collected sources of data. Organizations can also participate in broader surveys that include multiple organizations in the sample for external benchmarking purposes for many organizational metrics. As with behavior change, organization-level results are affected by a number of factors, such as the broader economic and political environment, the financial standing of the organization, and changes in market demands. Furthermore, the role of ethics training in the relationship between ethical behaviors and organizational outcomes is complex. To illustrate, after the employees of a sales department take ethics training, the number of sales that year may decrease or be below average. However, customer satisfaction scores may simultaneously increase. This may be due to employees interacting with clients in ways congruent with certain ethical principles taught during training. A new, more ethical, approach to sales may result in the process of winning a client taking more time, but the relationship with the client is improved.

However, just because two variables are positively or negatively related to one another, this does not mean that one variable *causes* the other to occur. Alternate explanations for outcomes should be considered and need to be ruled out. Organizational metrics obtained before training was implemented can be compared with those same metrics obtained once training has become well-established in the organization. When making this comparison, it is important to take into account other factors that might influence changes in these metrics over time, such as the imposition of new organizational regulations or shifts in the broader social environment. It is difficult to say with certainty whether an ethics training program is truly the cause of certain changes in organizational metrics. Therefore, it is important to exercise caution when discussing ethics training effectiveness and organization-level outcomes jointly.

How to use evaluation data

Below we describe how training evaluation data can be used in a number of ways that benefit the organization. However, with all of the benefits that ethics training program evaluation provides, certain privacy and confidentiality concerns need to be addressed. In particular, an individual's data bearing on a person's ethicality and ethical behavior are sensitive and, if not used appropriately, can cause harm to the individual whose data is being exploited. Therefore, it is essential that all ethics training evaluation data are handled in a confidential manner and that employees are made aware of this. A key mechanism to handling data confidentially is to de-identify the data so that individuals cannot be traced back to their responses and to report findings in aggregate.

Program development

Evaluation data can be used to inform the development and refinement of training content and delivery methods. Specifically, reaction data from training participants can be used to determine whether or not certain aspects of the training program require further change, updating, or improvement. For example, if reaction data or trainee comments suggest that aspects of training content are outdated, this content can be replaced with newer, more relevant content and examples.

Program marketing

Evaluation data can also be used to internally and externally market the effectiveness of the ethics training program to relevant stakeholders. Having data that provide evidence for training effectiveness, and qualitative reaction data or quotes, that convey trainees' positive perceptions of the training can help drum up interest in the ethics training and communicate its value.

Program effectiveness

Trainee performance on assessments, such as knowledge, skill, or attitudinal assessments, can help managers take a diagnostic approach to whether or not the ethics training program achieves its stated learning objectives. Because the evaluation measures administered should be linked directly to the learning objectives of the training, trainee performance on these measures can be a quality indicator of whether trainees have improved or have met a minimum level of competence as a result of having taken training. If trainees do not perform on these measures as expected, this signals a need to examine potential reasons for the ineffectiveness of training. Trainees may have already performed well on the measure prior to taking training, limiting the opportunity for much improvement to take place. It may also take time for training to have its intended effect on certain outcomes, which may partly explain limited performance gains on the part of trainees. Regardless of the type of assessment used, trainee performance on the assessment can be used as an indicator of training effectiveness if done so systematically and thoughtfully.

Organizational effects

In an ideal world, it would be easy and quick to demonstrate the effect of ethics training on organizational outcomes, such as a reduction in the number of ethical scandals or ethics complaints or improvements in employee performance. However, these outcomes are influenced by a confluence of factors, often beyond the control of managers (e.g., factors external to the organization). When ethics trainings do have an effect on these organization-level outcomes, it may take an extended amount of time for these changes to take form. When trying to demonstrate to upper management the value of ethics training programs, it is important to keep these challenges in mind. To demonstrate that ethics training is worth an investment of organizational resources, showing data on trainee reactions and performance on evaluation measures is a viable approach. Additionally, showing insights from past research on the impact of ethics training can demonstrate a training's potential value (see Chapter 3).

Ethics training evaluation data can also be used to detect the occurrence of ethical issues or blind spots within an organization. Specifically, if certain employees, for instance in a particular team or department, perform a certain way on a measure, this signals that the team or department may have a greater proclivity toward certain ethical behavioral or decision-making tendencies. This information can then be used to develop additional interventions targeted toward addressing these tendencies.

Individual feedback

Caution should be exercised when distributing an individual's data on ethics training evaluation performance. Organizations should be transparent to their employees about how individual data will be used. Data can be used for developmental purposes and for making certain personnel decisions. Performance on these measures should be used very carefully and judiciously for personnel decisions (e.g., performance appraisal), such that the measures used are legally defensible and directly job-relevant. However, there are other, rarer cases where an organization might use individual-level data to make personnel decisions. For example, if an employee self-reports on a measure that they have broken the law, the organization would have grounds for an investigation and possible termination of employment. Similarly, organizations might be justified in holding back a manager who has been reported for unethical conduct on multiple occasions. Individual feedback can also be provided directly to employees for developmental purposes. With this, employees should be provided with information to help them interpret this feedback. However, as mentioned earlier in the chapter, when publicly reporting data, it should be analyzed and reported at an aggregated, de-identified level to protect employee confidentiality.

Conclusion

Much like making the decision to buy or build a house, planning the evaluation approach for an ethics training program requires a number of critical considerations.

- What assessments suit your ethics training program the best?
- Will you build an assessment from scratch?
- Will you use existing assessments?
- How do you plan to use the assessments?

As with buying a new house and deciding on every specification, building a new assessment may provide more opportunities for increased customization but comes at the expense of increased time, resources, and headaches. Ethics training administrators must weigh the costs and benefits of building a custom assessment versus using an existing assessment and select the option best suited for the needs of their training program.

While it is important to acknowledge that no single evaluation measure will provide a complete picture of ethics training effectiveness, evaluation should be done systematically and regularly. Moreover, evaluation is based on a pattern of findings. Therefore, it will be important to ask yourself, Do I have a complete picture of training effectiveness? and Will these results hold up over time? Evaluation should be done not to just 'check the box,' rather, it should be done with the intent of utility. Information from ethics training program evaluation can be used to improve the content and processes of ethics training programs and provide information about whether or not the training program has the intended effects on trainees and related outcomes. In sum, training evaluation is a valuable tool managers can use to assess training effectiveness and demonstrate its utility.

References

Antes, A., & DuBois, J. M. (2014). Aligning objectives and assessment in responsible conduct of research instruction. *Journal of Microbiology & Biology Education, 15*, 108–116.

Antes, A. L., Thiel, C. E., Martin, L. E., Stenmark, C. K., Connelly, S., Devenport, L. D., & Mumford, M. D. (2012). Applying cases to solve ethical problems: The significance of positive and process-oriented reflection. *Ethics & Behavior, 22*, 113–130.

Arce, D. G., & Gentile, M. C. (2015). Giving voice to values as a leverage point in business ethics education. *Journal of Business Ethics, 131*, 535–542.

Bennett, R. J., & Robinson, S. L. (2000). Development of a measure of workplace deviance. *Journal of Applied Psychology, 85*, 349–360.

Boateng, G. O., Neilands, T. B., Frongillo, E. A., Melgar-Quinonez, H. R., & Young, S. L. (2018). Best practices for developing and validating scales for health, social, and behavioral research: A primer. *Frontiers in Public Health, 6*, 1–18.

Cohen, J. (1992). A power primer. *Psychological Bulletin, 112*, 155–159.

Clevenger, J., Pereira, G. M., Wiechmann, D., Schmitt, N., & Harvey, V. S. (2001). Incremental validity of situational judgment tests. *Journal of Applied Psychology, 86*, 410–417.

Cullen, J. B., Vic tor, B., & Bronson, J. W. (1993). The ethical climate questionnaire: An assessment of its development and validity. *Psychological Reports, 73,* 667–674.

Deloitte, & Compliance Week. (2016). In focus: 2016 compliance trends survey. Retrieved on January 15, 2019 from https://www2.deloitte.com/content/dam/Deloitte/us/Documents/governance-risk-compliance/us-advisory-compliance-week-survey.pdf

DuBois, J. M., Chibnall, J. T., Tait, R. C., Vander Wal, J. S., Baldwin, K. A., Antes, A. L., & Mumford, M. D. (2016). Professional decision-making in research (PDR): The validity of a new measure. *Science and Engineering Ethics, 22,* 391–416.

Gentile, M. C. (2012). Values-driven leadership development: Where we have been and where we could go. *Organization Management Journal, 9,* 188–196.

Goldstein, I. L. (1980). Training in work organizations. *Annual Review of Psychology, 31,* 229–272.

Goldstein, I. L., & Ford, J. K. (2002). *Training in organizations* (4th ed.). Belmont, CA: Wadsworth Cengage Learning.

Kirkpatrick, D. (1996). Great ideas revisited. *Training and Development, 50,* 54–59.

Kirkpatrick, D. L. (1983). Four steps to measuring training effectiveness. *Personnel Administrator, 28,* 19–25.

Kraiger, K., Ford, J. K., & Salas, E. (1993). Application of cognitive, skill-based, and affective theories of learning outcomes to new methods of training evaluation. *Journal of Applied Psychology, 78,* 311–328.

Messick, S. (1995). Validity of psychological assessment: Validation of inferences from persons' responses and performances as scientific inquiry into score meaning. *American Psychologist, 50,* 741–749.

Mumford, M. D., Devenport, L. D., Brown, R. P., Connelly, S., Murphy, S. T., Hill, J. H., & Antes, A. L. (2006). Validation of ethical decision making measures: Evidence for a new set of measures. *Ethics & Behavior, 16,* 319–345.

Mumford, M. D., Connelly, S., Brown, R. P., Murphy, S. T., Hill, J. H., Antes, A. L., Waples, E. P., & Devenport, L. D. (2008). A sensemaking approach to ethics training for scientists: Preliminary evidence of training effectiveness. *Ethics & Behavior, 18,* 315–339.

Mumford, M. D., Steele, L., & Watts, L. L. (2015). Evaluating ethics education programs: A multilevel approach. *Ethics & Behavior, 25,* 37–60.

Noe, R. A. (2013). *Employee training and development.* New York, NY: McGraw Hill.

Ricker, K. L. (2006). Setting cut-scores: A critical review of the Angoff and modified Angoff methods. *Alberta Journal of Educational Research, 52,* 53–64.

Spector, P. E., & Fox, S. (2005). The stressor–emotion model of counterproductive work behavior. In S. Fox & P. Spector (Eds.), *Counterproductive work behavior: Investigations of actors and targets* (pp. 151–174). Washington, DC: American Psychological Association.

Steele, L. M., Mulhearn, T. J., Medeiros, K. E., Watts, L. L., Connelly, S., & Mumford, M. D. (2016). How do we know what works? A review and critique of current practices in ethics training evaluation. *Accountability in Research, 23,* 319–350.

Turner, M. R., Watts, L. L., Steele, L. M., Mulhearn, T. J., Torrence, B. S., Todd, E. M., Mumford, M. D., & Connelly, S. (2018). How did you like this course? The advantages and limitations of reaction criteria in ethics education. *Ethics & Behavior, 28,* 483–496.

Watts, L. L., Medeiros, K. E., McIntosh, T. J., & Mulhearn, T. J. (2020). *Decision biases in the context of ethics: Initial scale development and validation. Personality & Individual Differences.* doi:10.1016/j.paid.2019.109609

Watts, L. L., Medeiros, K. E., Mulhearn, T. J., Steele, L. M., Connelly, S., & Mumford, M. D. (2017). Are ethics training programs improving? A meta-analytic review of past and present ethics instruction in the sciences. *Ethics & Behavior, 27,* 351–384.

Watts, L. L., Todd, E. M., Mulhearn, T. J., Medeiros, K. E., Mumford, M. D., & Connelly, S. (2017). Qualitative evaluation methods in ethics education: A systematic review and analysis of best practices. *Accountability in Research, 24,* 225–242.

7

TRAINING CONTENT

Tyler J. Mulhearn

***

Few topics evoke such a wide range of perspectives and opinions as ethics. The study of ethics is thousands of years old and has been discussed and debated in religious institutions, university lecture halls, corporate board rooms, and government offices. Not only do ethical principles span millennia and pervade institutions in various domains, but specific professional fields also have differing norms, expectations, and rules. Beyond these complicating factors, novel, complex, and ambiguous ethical issues are constantly emerging in today's interconnected global economy. With such a broad variety of ethical perspectives, how does one begin to reconcile these numerous perspectives to determine the most optimal or appropriate approach for their ethics training program?

One viable answer is to suggest ethics training content should be determined by the objectives established for the training program, as established by thorough analysis of the organization's unique constraints, resources, and needs (see Chapter 5). Ultimately, the development of any training program, ethics or otherwise, should rely on systematic decision making where the components fit together like a puzzle (Goldstein & Ford, 2002). Nevertheless, in practice, decisions about what content to cover in ethics training can seem ambiguous, and at times, maybe even over-whelming.

Diversity of perspectives and choices

To identify common goals of ethics training programs, Kalichman and Plemmons (2007) interviewed 50 research ethics instructors. These interviews resulted in over 50 unique reported goals of ethics training, including promoting compliance with regulations, ethical decision-making skills, responsibility to society, and communication with others. Beyond these reported goals, specific topics such as data management, conflicts of interest, misconduct, and whistleblowing were also reported as common topics.

Not surprisingly, the lack of consensus in training topics is not limited to the area of research ethics. Ethics training programs in business schools and organizations also cover a variety of topics. Indeed, in a meta-analysis that reviewed over 40 business ethics training programs, it was found that the most frequently reported topics included moral philosophy, social responsibility, contemporary ethical issues, responsibility to stakeholders, and legal issues (Medeiros et al., 2017). These five topic areas illustrate the diversity and range in instructional approaches used in business schools and organizations. At one level, this instructional diversity is unsurprising given the ethical scandals of the early 2000s and the subsequent pressure to implement corrective actions. The increased pressure to implement corrective actions was naturally intertwined with a diversity of perspectives on the 'best way' to teach ethics. For example, Christensen, Peirce, Hartman, Hoffman, and Carrier (2007) interviewed deans and directors of 50 top MBA programs and found an increase in the number of ethics programs and interest in these programs in comparison to a similar survey in 1988. This increased need and desire for ethics training programs very well may have provoked the inception of many programs and instructional approaches.

The decisions about what training content to include should not be taken lightly given the considerable range of effectiveness in ethics training programs (Watts et al., 2017). In other words, training content may be a primary cause of why some training programs are more effective than others. Moreover, a lack of demonstrated effectiveness may result in wasted time and money on the part of organizational leaders, ethics training managers, trainers, and trainees. Any organizational initiative requires substantial resources to greenlight and implement such an effort. As a result, a demonstration of the potential return on investment of a training program can help alleviate the skepticism of key organizational decision makers.

So what content should be included in an ethics training program? The answer to this question is not straightforward. As should be clear by now, the development of an effective ethics training program requires thoughtful analysis and diligent creativity. The purpose of this chapter is to provide a general overview of the primary instructional content approaches for ethics training.

Content framework

When developing an ethics training program and developing an instructional framework, an ethics training manager must determine the goals and intent of the training program. For one, it can be assumed that an organization is investing resources and time into an ethics training program for the same reason it expends resources and time for any product or service. That is, ethics can be viewed as a problem, similar to any other business problem, that needs to be solved (Noe, 2013). The goal of many ethics training programs, thus, focuses on improving trainees' capabilities to solve ethical problems. Although other potential goals such as changing the ethical culture or reporting wrongdoing may exist, developing the capacity to solve ethical problems is generally the primary intent of most ethics training programs. Organizations can accomplish this in multiple ways, including improving ethical knowledge or problem-solving skills of trainees.

Once the objectives of ethics training are established, the ethics training manager must then decide what approach or perspective is most useful for his or her ethics training program. To facilitate this decision-making process, a framework or model of instructional content is beneficial for organizing the variety of perspectives in ethics training content and can be useful as an initial starting point for gaining familiarity with the various types of instructional content. To provide a useful framework that applies to multiple disciplines, the framework must include components generalizable across disciplines. In other words, these components must not be limited to the unique considerations of a particular field or set of fields. One elegant framework that has been proposed in recent years is the Giving Voice to Values (GVV) curriculum (Arce & Gentile, 2015). The GVV curriculum discusses three types of instructional content: Awareness, Analysis, and Action.

Proponents of the GVV curriculum note that most ethics training programs traditionally emphasize the Awareness and Analysis components while placing less emphasis on the Action component. The authors of this book adopt the perspective that all three components are fundamental to the effective resolution of ethical problems. To solve any ethical problem, one must be *aware* of the key issues, parties, and constraints involved; *analyze* how different actions might result in different outcomes for stakeholders; and *act* once a decision is made. For the remainder of this chapter, we will discuss these three components in greater detail and discuss a framework that can help guide the selection of content for ethics training programs. Table 7.1 presents a list of exemplar ethics training programs that have applied Awareness, Analysis, and Action content.

Awareness

To resolve an ethical problem, one must first be aware that a problem exists. Further, the individual should identify the key issues, parties involved, constraints, and challenges related to the ethical problem. In the scientific literature, this area of study is typically referred to as ethical sensitivity (Shawver & Sennetti, 2009). Regardless of the type of problem one encounters, ethical or otherwise, a failure to properly identify and define the problem to be solved will result in a suboptimal outcome (Reiter-Palmon & Robinson, 2009). To demonstrate ethical sensitivity, one must recognize the complexities of ethical issues and how they may impact the personal and professional lives of other stakeholders (Clarkeburn, 2002). Thus, ethical awareness requires that the individual be sensitive to how ethical problems can impact others and possess relevant knowledge of field-specific issues.

Table 7.1 Exemplar Programs for Three Types of Training Content

Program Type and Source	Overview	Content	Delivery
Awareness: Cho and Shin (2014)	Hybrid 30-hour course for nursing students intended to increase self-directed learning	Bioethics, research ethics, research misconduct, publication ethics and copyright, collaborative research, and conflict of interest	Online delivery, small group lecture, discussion, case study
Awareness: Ramalingam, Bhuvaneswari, and SanKaRan (2014)	1-day ethics workshop for medical faculty	History and principles of ethics, confidentiality, conflicts of interest, publication ethics	Lecture, group discussion
Analysis: Mumford et al. (2008)	2-day professional workshop intended to improve ethical decision-making skills of graduate students	Decision-making strategies, sensemaking	Cases, lecture, group discussion, role play
Analysis: DuBois, Chibnall, Tait, and Vander Wal (2018)	3-day workshop intended to remediate researchers found to violate rules or regulations	Decision-making strategies, biases, norms, stress	Lecture, group discussion, professional development plan, pre- and post-workshop activities
Action: Chappell, Webb, and Edwards (2011)	12-week MBA course focused on improving students' capacity to act effectively in ethics situations	Giving Voice to Values, biases, whistleblowing	Case studies, reflection activities, team project
Action: Seiler, Fischer, and Voegtli (2011)	1-week training program for Swiss Military Academy	Realistic job scenarios, solutions and reflections on scenarios	Cases, group discussion

Ethical sensitivity necessitates constant vigilance and monitoring to identify any potential ethical problems emerging in the environment. As such, scanning one's environment for irregularities or unexpected actions by others may be the first step to identifying an ethical problem (Thiel, Bagdasarov, Harkrider, Johnson, & Mumford, 2012). Acknowledging that ethical issues may emerge at any time from any individual, team, or department is critical to ethical sensitivity. This is not to suggest that employees should act as if they are paranoid special detectives, attempting to track down their organization's next big ethical problem. Instead, employees should remain alert on a day-to-day basis and recognize that unexpected parties, such as their closest colleagues and friends, could be ethical transgressors. Moreover, employees must remain vigilant of their own biases and decision-making tendencies to limit the chances that one finds him or herself mired in an ethical issue (Watts, Medeiros, McIntosh, & Mulhearn, 2020). Engaging in periodic self-reflection can improve capacities to resolve ethical dilemmas as they arise (DuBois et al., 2018; Sekerka, Godwin, & Charnigo, 2014).

Ethical sensitivity extends beyond abstract conceptualizations of imagined figures and problems. Rather, it involves a clear understanding of organizational or field-based rules, guidelines, and expectations one must abide by in his or her professional life (Trevino, Weaver, Gibson, & Toffler, 1999). Thus, ethical sensitivity, as it relates to field-specific issues, involves compliance with mandated standards or regulations as well as adherence to field norms.

To comply with mandated standards or regulations, one must possess considerable knowledge of those standards and regulations. Not surprisingly, field-specific standards and regulations vary considerably from one field to another (Mulhearn, Watts, et al., 2017). This point, while it may be obvious, reinforces the importance of training individuals on the specific content they need to know in their field, profession, or job to navigate challenging ethical issues.

As a result, in applying a field-specific approach to ethics training content, managers must identify and explain the key issues relevant to their target audience. Depending on the organization or field involved, a code of conduct may exist which explicitly details the fundamental issues professionals will face in their careers (Babri, Davidson, & Helin, 2018). However, codes of conduct can be dry and full of 'legalese,' making their incorporation into a palatable ethics training program difficult. An important challenge for the ethics training manager is to seamlessly integrate the code of conduct into the training program in a manner that keeps the trainees engaged, while still communicating the key points (Harkrider et al., 2012).

Although codes of conduct are beneficial for understanding key ethical issues, it should be recognized that these documents are not set in stone. Despite the enduring nature of many ethical issues, new issues may emerge in the future. For instance, the integration of information technology within our daily work and non-work lives has become much more prevalent today compared to 20 years ago. As a result, ethical issues surrounding data privacy, sharing, and confidentiality have become increasingly important (Russell, Hauert, Altman, & Veloso, 2015). Thus, ethics training managers and employees must be cognizant of emerging ethical issues in their field. The capacity to identify or even forecast novel ethical issues can facilitate greater ethical sensitivity and contribute to better ethical decision-making skills (Stenmark et al., 2010).

Analysis

Gaining awareness that an ethical problem exists is not sufficient for solving that problem. An individual, or team, must analyze the objectives and interests of involved parties as well as key aspects of the situation to effectively solve ethical problems (Mumford et al., 2008). Unlike other types of routine problems that frequently occur in organizations, ethical issues can at times be complex, ambiguous, and ill-defined (Sonenshein, 2007). Because of this complexity, individuals who are skilled at breaking down ethical issues into their essential components are more likely to arrive at an ethical solution that satisfies key stakeholders.

On the other hand, in many cases, ethical issues are straightforward and ethical solutions will be obvious to most employees and easy to implement. These more straightforward ethical issues tend to receive less attention in programs focused on building analytic capabilities, because substantial analysis is not required to reach ethical solutions to simple issues. In cases where a clear solution to an ethical problem is apparent, the more critical issue is the implementation of these decisions into effective actions, which will be discussed further in the next section. In contrast, ethics training programs that incorporate analysis content tend to emphasize the strategies that employees can use to solve more complex problems.

Researchers sometimes refer to the process of analyzing ethical issues as sensemaking. Sensemaking involves identifying and integrating relevant information to generate potential solutions to a complex problem (Weick, 1995). Types of relevant information may include personal concerns, interpersonal expectations, situational constraints, and general norms relevant to the ethical problem (Mumford, Friedrich, Caughron, & Antes, 2009). Integrating these sources of information enables individuals to understand what is important and what is unimportant in an ethical issue. Not surprisingly, individuals who possess more experience relevant to the problem they are facing benefit more from sensemaking. Experience may be used to understand and organize various types of situations that one may encounter in life. Based on prior experience, one can predict how future situations are likely to unfold and act based on this information (Dörner & Schaub, 1994).

Of course, the situation one is facing today may not perfectly match up with past experience, but analogies can be drawn, and similar principles can be applied to reach an ethical solution. In ethics training programs, encouraging reflection on trainees' prior experiences can be leveraged as a resource. Such knowledge can provide trainees with relevant information about the key causes, goals, principles, emotions, and other factors involved in ethical issues (Thiel et al., 2012). However, trainee knowledge is, of course, not limited to their own experiences. Providing trainees with cases, or short narratives involving characters that face ethical issues, is another way to build experience so trainees are well-equipped to handle complex issues should they emerge in the future. To draw an analogy, athletes at all levels practice multiple times per week not only to increase their skills but also to be more prepared for actual game situations where pressure and scrutiny is magnified. Similarly, trainees who have more practice analyzing ethical issues relevant to their work are more likely to execute appropriately when facing ethical issues on the job. Although practice can never make perfect, it certainly makes for a better athlete or ethical decision maker.

Sensemaking is supported not only by knowledge and experience, but also by a few key strategies that have been shown to facilitate ethical decision making. Thiel et al. (2012) proposed four key strategies that support ethical sensemaking by leaders in organizations: emotion regulation, self-reflection, forecasting, and information integration. First, given that emotions tend to be high in ethical situations, training employees to better regulate their emotions can facilitate more rational decisions. Some strategies for emotion regulation include reappraising one's thoughts or modifying one's situation to improve objectivity (Gross, 2015). Second, training individuals on how to analyze previous successes and failures through self-reflection can also support sensemaking. Third, training individuals in forecasting, or the process of considering the likely outcomes associated with different decisions, can help people learn to anticipate how their actions may affect themselves and others (Mumford, Schultz, & Van Doorn, 2001). Fourth, it is critical to train individuals to integrate these complex sources of information such that ethical solutions become more likely. Integration involves organizing or reworking information into a coherent summary or narrative that translates into a viable action plan.

Although various approaches to analyzing ethical problems exist, the preceding discussion summarizes several key elements found to be effective for ethical problem solving in many professional fields and settings. By helping trainees acquire the right kinds of knowledge and skills, they are more likely to make ethical decisions in the workplace. The recommendations suggested here also can help to limit the potential biases that may manifest in ethical situations by enhancing the objectivity of decisions (Bagdasarov et al., 2016). A more objective, rational approach can help to improve the quality of ethical decisions and outcomes for all parties involved.

Action

A common misconception is that the topic of ethics is too theoretical and abstract to inform 'real-world' decisions. Of course, this is not the case. Ethical decision making in organizations is tangible and requires deliberate action. Thus, an emphasis on how to *act* on ethical decisions in actual work situations when the time is appropriate is beneficial, if not critical, for ethics training programs. This is not only the case for complex ethical issues, as described previously, but also for issues with a straightforward solution requiring implementation. After one has become aware of and analyzed an ethical problem, decisions must be formulated and acted upon. This may be easier said than done, as action plans do not always translate into behavior (Ajzen, 2011). Organizational politics and conflicting interests among stakeholders can thwart even the best-laid plans. These organizational realities reinforce the need for employees to be fully prepared to act with wisdom and tact in response to ethical issues.

The GVV curriculum is one example of an ethics training approach that emphasizes 'post-decision making,' or how trainees can go about implementing their decisions (Gentile, 2013). In action-oriented programs, trainees may be asked to craft action plans that consider how their decisions might actually be carried out in practice. Action plans include a number of elements, such as stakeholders and their interests, main perspectives to be considered or countered in carrying out the plan, and how to influence others who disagree with the agreed-upon approach (Arce & Gentile, 2015). Training in action-based practices is beneficial because ethical decision making ultimately involves carrying out decisions in a social context involving parties with varying interests and opinions. When implementing a decision that affects others, one must be prepared to build support and influence others.

Forecasting, or considering future consequences, is a key skill involved in crafting successful implementation plans. Thus, it is beneficial to have trainees practice forecasting the considerations of key parties and the steps that one might take to effectively influence these parties. For example, identifying the perspectives of other individuals while attempting to argue for one's own perspective may prove critical to minimizing the possibility of allowing an ethical issue to snowball into a much larger problem.

A variety of delivery methods can be used to support the development of action planning skills in ethics training. For example, role-play simulations of ethical issues can allow trainees to practice influencing particular stakeholders in a low-stakes environment in real time. In these role plays, trainees can work together to formulate an action plan on how to influence skeptical stakeholders on how to resolve an ethical issue (Gentile, 2012). Content focused on self-reflection—such as responding to questions about stakeholders and situational elements involved in prior experiences—can also support trainee action planning. Finally, in-basket tasks where trainees respond to a variety of ethical situations and priorities in a simulated work scenario could also prove fruitful for allowing employees to practice crafting and carrying out action plans (e.g., Medeiros & Watts, 2020).

Awareness-Analysis-Action (AAA) framework

A large body of research supports the conclusion that content focused on awareness, analysis, and action are all valuable elements to incorporate in ethics training. However, in a review of ethics training programs, it was found that most ethics training programs tend to focus on only one of these aspects (Mulhearn, Steele, et al., 2017). Compared to programs that emphasize one type of content, the handful of ethics training programs that have effectively integrated multiple types of content tend to deliver uncharacteristically positive results.

One example of integration can be found in a model proposed to guide research ethics training in the biomedical sciences (Mumford et al., 2016). In this model, two major types of content were identified, including field-specific compliance and professional decision making. According to the model, when both types of content are effectively integrated in the same training program, effects on trainee ethical decision making are enhanced. In the present chapter, we extend this model beyond the context of bio-medical ethics to argue for the value of integrating content focused on awareness, analysis, and action in organizational ethics training programs more generally. For convenience, we refer to this model as the Awareness-Analysis-Action (AAA) framework. The AAA framework is illustrated in Figure 7.1.

The AAA framework suggests that three types of content—awareness, analysis, and action—merit inclusion in ethics training programs. Each of these types of content can deliver unique and complementary benefits that

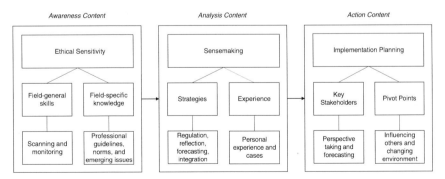

Figure 7.1 Awareness-Analysis-Action (AAA) Framework of Ethics Training Content.

support improvements in trainee ethical decision making. Although training content should ultimately be informed by the objectives of the program, the most effective programs seamlessly integrate all three types of content.

As may be seen in Figure 7.1, the framework consists of three major boxes representing each type of content—awareness, analysis, and action. Within each box, the fundamental aspects of each training approach are summarized. When confronting an ethical issue, it is not uncommon for awareness to precede analysis, which precedes action. Thus, this general sequence is represented in the framework.

In the awareness box, ethical sensitivity is the overarching content area of importance, with field-general and field-specific concerns involved. The field-general aspects of ethical sensitivity consist of scanning and monitoring, which are two key skills required to identify ethical issues regardless of one's professional field (Mumford, Steele, Mulhearn, McIntosh, & Watts, 2017). Scanning involves actively searching one's environment for information, contingencies, and challenges that may be pertinent to solving an ethical problem (McIntosh et al., 2016). Monitoring involves an ongoing assessment of current operational conditions (Mumford & Mulhearn, 2019). These two skills allow individuals to maintain a vigilant eye on potential emerging ethical issues. Scanning and monitoring are presented as 'general' ethical skills because these capabilities support ethical problem solving across organizations, fields, and industries.

Beyond scanning and monitoring, there are certain ethical policies or practices that are so widely accepted that they support ethical sensitivity in many fields. For example, the Belmont report provides universal guidelines on how to ethically conduct scientific research including maximizing benefit and minimizing harm. To provide another example, the Federal Trade Commission enforces Truth in Advertising laws, which require companies of all industries and sizes to provide truthful information in their advertisements and not mislead potential consumers. Universal laws or guidelines regarding appropriate behavior can provide a foundation for ethics training content that may be broadly applicable.

Field-specific aspects of ethical sensitivity, meanwhile, consist of field guidelines and norms, as well as emerging issues unique to the profession of trainees. Field guidelines and norms may be obtained from codes of conduct or other documents published by the profession. Emerging field issues can be identified in current market trends, research publications, and the introduction of innovative products and services. A core aspect of professional responsibility in any field is to keep apprised of emerging issues involving changes to field guidelines or norms.

In the analysis box, sensemaking is the primary content area of importance, with sensemaking strategies and experience as critical subcomponents. As previously discussed, example strategies that support sensemaking include regulating emotions, reflecting on personal motives and potential biases, forecasting potential consequences, and integrating information into a coherent narrative (Thiel et al., 2012). Practicing these cross-cutting strategies can facilitate sensemaking and improve ethical decision making regardless of the specific field or industry of trainees. Presenting trainees with cases featuring ethical issues relevant to their field is an effective approach to practicing these strategies and building field-specific knowledge. Thus, training programs that focus on strategies and relevant cases can be used to improve trainees' analytical capabilities that facilitate ethical decision making.

Finally, as illustrated in the action box, implementation planning is the primary content area of importance. Implementation planning involves identifying key stakeholders and their perspectives as well as pivot points for implementing ethical decisions. Relevant stakeholders include the relevant parties, within and outside of one's immediate circle or organization, that need to be considered in enacting an ethical decision. Stakeholders may include coworkers, subordinates, supervisors, customers, suppliers, the general public, the environment, or others. Given that different stakeholders likely hold different interests and perspectives, perspective-taking is a critical component of implementation planning. Additionally, forecasting the likely consequences of decisions for different stakeholder groups supports effective implementation planning. In addition to stakeholder considerations, identifying pivot points is also critical to implementation planning. Pivot points are elements of action plans where trainees must alter, or 'pivot,' to allow the decision to see the light of day. Example pivot points include influencing others to build support for a decision and gathering relevant documentation required to facilitate ethical action. By acting on such factors in one's environment, it allows the trainee to learn how to 'shift the scales' to achieve more ethical outcomes.

Conclusion

In this chapter, we reviewed three major approaches to ethics training content and provided a framework for guiding managers who are responsible for selecting training content. A few limitations should be noted when considering these recommendations. First, the framework proposed in this chapter should not be viewed as a panacea for ethics training content woes. Managers should consider the unique needs of their training population and organization based on an organizational analysis and should develop or adapt appropriate ethics training content accordingly. Second, the exemplar programs discussed in this chapter were described to illustrate how each training content approach has been implemented in real ethics training programs. Blind application of the specific content used in training programs in other contexts is not recommended. Third, although the AAA framework identifies the three primary types of content covered in ethics training programs, we did not discuss all of the more specific topics that may be included in ethics training.

With these limitations in mind, the AAA framework can serve as a guide for selecting what content to include in ethics training programs. Awareness content focuses on improving trainees' knowledge and skills that support the identification of ethical problems through enhanced ethical sensitivity. The goal of analysis content is to support sensemaking by practicing cross-cutting strategies and learning from experience. Finally, action content emphasizes the development of skills that support the planning and implementation of ethical decisions and provide the decision maker with the confidence to make ethical decisions in real-world scenarios. The AAA framework illustrates how awareness, analysis, and action content can work together to improve the effectiveness of ethics training in organizations.

References

Ajzen, I. (2011). The theory of planned behaviour: Reactions and reflections. *Psychology and Health, 26,* 1113–1127.

Arce, D. G., & Gentile, M. C. (2015). Giving voice to values as a leverage point in business ethics education. *Journal of Business Ethics, 131,* 535–542.

Babri, M., Davidson, B., & Helin, S. (2018). An updated inquiry into the study of corporate codes of ethics: 2005–2016. *Journal of Business Ethics*, 1–38. https://doi.org/10.1007/s10551-019-04192-x.

Bagdasarov, Z., Johnson, J. F., MacDougall, A. E., Steele, L. M., Connelly, S., & Mumford, M. D. (2016). Mental models and ethical decision making: The mediating role of sensemaking. *Journal of Business Ethics*, *138*, 133–144.

Chappell, S., Webb, D., & Edwards, M. (2011). A required GVV ethics course: Conscripting ethical conversations. *Journal of Business Ethics Education*, *8*, 308–319.

Cho, K. C., & Shin, G. (2014). Operational effectiveness of blended e-learning program for nursing research ethics. *Nursing Ethics*, *21*, 484–495.

Christensen, L. J., Peirce, E., Hoffman, W. M., & Carrier, J. (2007). Ethics, CSR, and sustainability education in the "Financial times" top 50 global business schools: Baseline data and future research directions. *Journal of Business Ethics*, *73*, 347–368.

Clarkeburn, H. (2002). A test for ethical sensitivity in science. *Journal of Moral Education*, *31*, 439–453.

Dörner, D., & Schaub, H. (1994). Errors in planning and decision-making and the nature of human information processing. *Applied Psychology*, *43*, 433–453.

DuBois, J. M., Chibnall, J. T., Tait, R., & Vander Wal, J. S. (2018). The professionalism and integrity in research program: Description and preliminary outcomes. *Academic Medicine*, *93*, 586–592.

Gentile, M. C. (2012). Values-driven leadership development: Where we have been and where we could go. *Organization Management Journal*, *9*, 188–196.

Gentile, M. C. (2013). *Educating for values-driven leadership: Giving voice to values across the curriculum*. New York, NY: Business Expert Press.

Goldstein, I. L., & Ford, J. K. (2002). *Training in organizations* (4th ed.). Belmont, CA: Wadsworth Cengage Learning.

Gross, J. J. (2015). Emotion regulation: Current status and future prospects. *Psychological Inquiry*, *26*, 1–26.

Harkrider, L. N., Thiel, C. E., Bagdasarov, Z., Mumford, M. D., Johnson, J. F., Connelly, S., & Devenport, L. D. (2012). Improving case-based ethics training with codes of conduct and forecasting content. *Ethics & Behavior*, *22*, 258–280.

Kalichman, M. W., & Plemmons, D. K. (2007). Reported goals for responsible conduct of research courses. *Academic Medicine*, *82*, 846–852.

McIntosh, T., Mulhearn, T., Gibson, C., Mumford, M. D., Yammarino, F. J., Connelly, S., Day, E. A., & Vessey, W. B. (2016). Planning for long-duration space exploration: Interviews with NASA subject matter experts. *Acta Astronautica, 129,* 477–487.

Medeiros, K. E., & Watts, L. L. (2020). An ethical leadership assessment center: Assessing and developing moral person and moral manager dimensions. Unpublished manuscript.

Medeiros, K. E., Watts, L. L., Mulhearn, T. J., Steele, L. M., Mumford, M. D., & Connelly, S. (2017). What is working, what is not, and what we need to know: A meta-analytic review of business ethics instruction. *Journal of Academic Ethics, 15,* 245–275.

Mulhearn, T. J., Steele, L. M., Watts, L. L., Medeiros, K. E., Mumford, M. D., & Connelly, S. (2017). Review of instructional approaches in ethics education. *Science and Engineering Ethics, 23,* 883–912.

Mulhearn, T. J., Watts, L. L., Torrence, B. S., Todd, E. M., Turner, M. R., Connelly, S., & Mumford, M. D. (2017). Cross-field comparison of ethics education: Golden rules and particulars. *Accountability in Research, 24,* 211–224.

Mumford, M. D., & Mulhearn, T. J. (2019). Leading creative research and development efforts: A literature review and proposed framework for the engineering domain. *Proceedings of the Institution of Mechanical Engineers, Part C: Journal of Mechanical Engineering Science, 233,* 403–414.

Mumford, M. D., Connelly, S., Brown, R. P., Murphy, S. T., Hill, J. H., Antes, A. L., Waples, E. P., & Devenport, L. D. (2008). A sensemaking approach to ethics training for scientists: Preliminary evidence of training effectiveness. *Ethics & Behavior, 18,* 315–339.

Mumford, M. D., Friedrich, T. L., Caughron, J. J., & Antes, A. L. (2009). Leadership research: Traditions, developments, and current directions. In D. Buchanan & A. Bryman (Eds.), *The Sage handbook of organizational research methods* (pp. 111–127). Thousand Oaks, CA: Sage Publications.

Mumford, M. D., Schultz, R. A., & Van Doorn, J. R. (2001). Performance in planning: Processes, requirements, and errors. *Review of General Psychology, 5,* 213–240.

Mumford, M. D., Steele, L., Mulhearn, T. J., McIntosh, T. J., & Watts, L. L. (2017). Leader planning skills and creative performance: Integrating past, present, and future. In M. D. Mumford & S. Hemlin (Eds.), *Handbook of research on leadership and creativity* (pp. 17–39). Cheltenham, UK: Elgar.

Mumford, M. D., Watts, L. L., Medeiros, K. E., Mulhearn, T. J., Steele, L. M., & Connelly, S. (2016). Biomedical ethics education may benefit from integrating compliance and analysis approaches. *Nature Immunology, 17*, 605–608.

Noe, R. A. (2013). *Employee training and development*. New York, NY: McGraw Hill.

Ramalingam, S., Bhuvaneswari, S., & SanKaRan, R. (2014). Ethics workshops: Are they effective in improving the competencies of faculty and post-graduates? *Journal of Clinical and Diagnostic Research, 8*, XC01–XC03.

Reiter-Palmon, R., & Robinson, E. J. (2009). Problem identification and construction: What do we know, what is the future? *Psychology of Aesthetics, Creativity, and the Arts, 3*, 43–47.

Russell, S., Hauert, S., Altman, R., & Veloso, M. (2015). Ethics of artificial intelligence. *Nature, 521*, 415–416.

Seiler, S., Fischer, A., & Voegtli, S. A. (2011). Developing moral decision-making competence: A quasi-experimental intervention study in the Swiss Armed Forces. *Ethics & Behavior, 21*, 452–470.

Sekerka, L. E., Godwin, L. N., & Charnigo, R. (2014). Motivating managers to develop their moral curiosity. *Journal of Management Development, 33*, 709–722.

Shawver, T. J., & Sennetti, J. T. (2009). Measuring ethical sensitivity and evaluation. *Journal of Business Ethics, 88*, 663–678.

Sonenshein, S. (2007). The role of construction, intuition, and justification in responding to ethical issues at work: The sensemaking-intuition model. *Academy of Management Review, 32*, 1022–1040.

Stenmark, C. K., Antes, A. L., Wang, X., Caughron, J. J., Thiel, C. E., & Mumford, M. D. (2010). Strategies in forecasting outcomes in ethical decision-making: Identifying and analyzing the causes of the problem. *Ethics & Behavior, 20*, 110–127.

Thiel, C. E., Bagdasarov, Z., Harkrider, L., Johnson, J. F., & Mumford, M. D. (2012). Leader ethical decision-making in organizations: Strategies for sensemaking. *Journal of Business Ethics, 107*, 49–64.

Trevino, L. K., Weaver, G. R., Gibson, D. G., & Toffler, B. L. (1999). Managing ethics and legal compliance: What works and what hurts. *California Management Review, 41*, 131–151.

Watts, L. L., Medeiros, K. E., McIntosh, T. J., & Mulhearn, T. J. (2020). *Decision biases in the context of ethics: Initial scale development and validation. Personality & Individual Differences.* doi:10.1016/j.paid.2019.109609.

Watts, L. L., Medeiros, K. E., Mulhearn, T. J., Steele, L. M., Connelly, S., & Mumford, M. D. (2017). Are ethics training programs improving? A meta-analytic review of past and present ethics instruction in the sciences. *Ethics & Behavior, 27*, 351–384.

Weick, K. E. (1995). *Sensemaking in organizations* (Vol. 3). Thousand Oaks, CA: Sage Publications.

8

DELIVERY METHODS

Tyler J. Mulhearn

***

Once a decision has been made about what content to include in a training program, the ethics training manager must decide how to deliver this content to trainees. To put it another way, if content is the cargo of training, delivery methods are the mode of transportation used to deliver the cargo. As with delivering cargo, a variety of options exist when it comes to deciding how to deliver content in a training program. Managers should not take this decision lightly as time, cost, and trainee learning are all impacted by the delivery methods employed. To add to this complexity, the decision generally does not boil down to *which* delivery method to use but rather *what combination* of delivery methods to use. To support this decision-making process, we provide an overview of the most commonly used delivery methods in ethics training. The chapter ends with a description of steps to follow in seamlessly integrating delivery methods into a training program.

Overview of delivery methods

Although there are multiple ways to distinguish various instructional approaches, one common distinction is between face-to-face and online instructional approaches. Face-to-face, or 'traditional,' training programs typically involve one or more trainers in a classroom setting instructing trainees on a single topic or multiple topics. Online training programs, meanwhile, involve instruction through a web-based resource. Although these two instructional approaches may appear rather dissimilar on the surface, specific delivery methods, such as discussions or cases, can often be adapted to either delivery method. Face-to-face and online instructional approaches can also complement one another by compensating for the shortcomings of the other approach. This combination will be discussed further in the Blended/hybrid instructional approach section. We will next discuss the specific components of the various instructional approaches and delivery methods that may be employed in ethics training.

Face-to-face instructional approach

Although commonly associated with lectures, face-to-face delivery should encompass more than a simple one-way communication of instructor to trainees. Rather, it should be an exchange of dialogue between instructor and trainees. Face-to-face delivery methods also include more active methods such as discussions, role plays, case-based learning, and team-based learning (Watts et al., 2017). Moreover, when one or more of these techniques are combined with lecturing, the effectiveness of the course is likely to increase dramatically by providing trainees with practice and feedback to reinforce key learning points (Goldstein & Ford, 2002). This is particularly true for a complex topic such as ethics.

Two pragmatic decisions for face-to-face training programs that need to be made are regarding the class size and setup (Noe, 2013). There are generally no strict rules of thumb regarding the optimal class size, so long as multiple delivery methods are used and trainees are actively engaged. However, the training room can be set up in such a manner that trainees are more likely to interact with one another by placing seats near each other. A setup of this nature will enable trainees to easily transition into group discussion following lecture or other activities. Next, we will discuss the various delivery methods that are commonly used in face-to-face training programs.

Lecture

Perhaps the most commonly used delivery method, lecture, involves a trainer delivering information to a group of trainees, typically in a face-to-face format. Lecture can be effective for providing significant amounts of information to a large group of trainees at a relatively low cost. Assuming the trainer is knowledgeable in the subject matter being taught, lecture is an efficient way to provide information to trainees. More commonly today, trainers are supplementing lectures with visual aids using programs like Microsoft PowerPoint or Prezi. Using visual aids can help combat some of the downsides to lecturing, such as its passive nature or lack of trainee involvement. However, visual aids do not necessarily translate into greater trainee engagement. Managers must ensure that learning principles are incorporated in order for visual aids to facilitate learning (Clark & Mayer, 2016). Within these visual aids, videos can be added to illustrate key points, or discussion questions can be embedded to facilitate discussion. For example, video skits may show characters demonstrating a learning concept already covered in the lecture. Short, relevant videos from movies or TV shows that illustrate key learning points also offer the benefit of providing an entertaining means of supplementing information covered in the lecture.

Discussion

The use of discussion provides trainees with the opportunity to provide their input on the subject matter and connect their personal experiences and worldview to training content. Doing so enables trainees to make greater meaning of training content. More importantly, when facilitating discussion, trainers should let trainees practice engaging with the material and should provide appropriate feedback to illustrate what trainees did correctly and incorrectly in a constructive manner. This allows trainees to practice and learn in a safe environment. One added benefit of such an approach is that other trainees may also contribute their unique perspectives to the discussion or learn vicariously by observing and listening to others. A potential disadvantage of discussion is the lack of control over what trainees might say, which may result in irrelevant or unproductive discussions. Trainers should make attempts to keep discussions on-topic.

Debate

A related delivery method that also allows trainees to engage in large group discussions is a debate. Trainees may be asked to participate on one of two, or more, sides of a debate for an ethical issue to better articulate and understand the key arguments of each side. One potential advantage of debates is that it allows trainees to engage in perspective taking, a key skill in ethical decision making (Mencl & May, 2009), by encouraging them to consider a perspective they had not considered previously. The potential downside to employing debates is that trainees may feel unenthusiastic, or worse, coerced, into adopting a perspective with which they strongly disagree. However, the likelihood of this occurring is rather low and may be mitigated by noting that the side for which one is arguing is not important but the general exercise of engaging in a debate on a complex issue is important for developing one's ethical decision-making skills. Moreover, the nature of the debate is also important, such that trainees should not simply be placed into an 'ethical side' and an 'unethical side.' A more fruitful approach would be to place trainees into multiple sides, two or more, that advocate for different ways of implementing an ethical decision (Gentile, 2012). This will help trainees to evaluate the pros and cons of different implementation strategies.

Role play

In contrast to general group discussion and debate, role plays allow trainees to adopt the roles of fictional characters in a hypothetical scenario. This approach provides the advantage of allowing trainees to act out a scenario they may encounter in the future without any of the repercussions of a real-life situation. This is particularly important in ethical scenarios given the complex social dynamics inherently involved when encountering ethical problems. As with discussion, the trainer should ensure that trainees are providing realistic responses and taking the scenario seriously. At the same time, it is okay to have some fun during role plays as some trainees may feel awkward acting out scenarios in front of their peers.

Providing scripts or background information of the characters should help keep trainee responses on course. Furthermore, asking trainees to rehearse the actions involved in implementing ethical decisions will likely benefit trainees in the long term by showing them how to enact the decision (Brummel, Gunsalus, Anderson, & Loui, 2010). Following the role play activity, trainees should have the opportunity to respond to the scenario. In addition, the trainer should summarize key learning points.

Case-based learning

Similar to role play scenarios, cases provide hypothetical scenarios, fictional or real, to illustrate key learning points. Rather than asking trainees to act out roles, cases are often portrayed in a written or video format. Cases provide trainees with the opportunity to practice the skills and knowledge they have gained throughout the training program. Like role plays, cases enable trainees to practice solving complex ethical issues with no clear, right-or-wrong solution. This practice facilitates effective problem solving in future, real-life ethical scenarios by illustrating what worked well and what did not in the case scenario. Trainees can work on ethical cases by themselves or work with a fellow trainee or small group. One benefit of working in pairs or small groups is that trainees are exposed to alternative viewpoints that they may not have considered on their own. These alternative viewpoints can help trainees better understand the various approaches to addressing an ethical problem that may be encountered in the future. Finally, whereas traditional cases have emphasized the early stages of the decision making (i.e., generating or analyzing a solution), case content is also available that emphasizes later stages of decision making (i.e., implementing a solution), such as encouraging the rehearsal of steps involved in taking ethical action (see Gentile, 2012).

In a review of delivery methods in ethics training, researchers identified case-based activities as one of four key themes of effective ethics training courses (Todd, Torrence, et al., 2017). Although cases can be effective delivery tools, they vary in terms of content, length, emotional content, and realism, among other factors (Bagdasarov, MacDougall, Johnson, & Mumford, 2015). Overall, research suggests that cases are more effective when they are longer but not overly complex (Watts et al., 2017). The likely reason for this is that it allows the training instructor to embed key learning principles and instructional content that relates directly to the interests and workplace scenarios of trainees.

Team-based learning

The potential for collaborating with others in ethics training points to another commonly used delivery method—team-based learning. With this delivery method, trainees form groups or teams at the beginning of training and work on exercises together throughout the program. Striking a balance between the number of individual and team-based activities is also beneficial (Todd, Torrence, et al., 2017).

The potential benefit of a team-based learning approach is increased trainee engagement by having trainees discuss ethical scenarios with one another rather than a large group. However, group-based exercises may lead shy or unengaged trainees to withdraw from training. To provide one example, while conducting an ethics training course, one of the authors of this book noticed a participant actively avoiding a group activity involving performing a skit. This training participant later informed the training instructors that he was not comfortable performing in front of large audiences. To increase learning for all trainees, ethics training instructors should establish a safe and supportive environment that increases the likelihood that all group members feel comfortable participating. For example, one common technique that may be employed is think-pair-share where individuals are asked to first think on their own, then pair up with a partner, then share with the larger group (Kaddoura, 2013).

Online instructional approach

The rise of emerging technologies makes it difficult to ignore the potential influence of technology on employee learning. Online training can be particularly attractive to organizations due to its low cost of administration, increased accessibility, and ease of tracking course completion. Thus, adopting online training programs for most, if not all, learning needs can be enticing (Brown, Murphy, & Wade, 2006). However, training programs that take place entirely online are unlikely to have their intended effect when complex skill acquisition, as in the case of ethics, is involved (Antes et al., 2009).

One reason for this lack of effectiveness is the common association of online ethics training with compliance training. To illustrate, it is much easier to deliver a training program that improves awareness of guidelines, rules, and regulations in an online format compared to an analysis-based training program. As discussed in Chapter 3, ethics training involves more than memorizing pre-specified guidelines, rules, and regulations (Weber & Wasieleski, 2013). Rather, ethics training, when conducted appropriately, prepares trainees for solving a range of ethical problems. Moreover, when trainees view training as another task on their to-do list rather than a fundamental aspect of their job, they are unlikely to invest time or reflect on critical concerns raised in the training course.

Despite the potential shortcomings of online training, ethics training managers can incorporate instructional design elements to improve the quality of the training program. To ensure that online trainings are beneficial, organizations should provide trainees with the time and space needed to complete the training. This may seem obvious, but trainees are more likely to pay attention to training materials when they have the time and energy to take part in a training program. This means that organizations should provide an appropriate amount of time for the trainee to complete the program. Similarly, organizations should invest resources into making a high-quality training program rather than designing a short, monotonous program to fulfill an industry requirement or government guideline.

Along with this, best practices in instructional design such as active learning, multiple instructional methods, practice, and feedback should be incorporated to ensure trainees are engaged and fully processing the information (Goldstein & Ford, 2002). If these elements are incorporated into the training program, the effectiveness of the program should greatly improve. In other words, just because a training program is online does not mean it needs to fit into the 'check-the-box' category. One example of an online program employing engaging content is the Social Cohort-Based program, which provides trainees with access to cases, animations and videos, and opportunities to practice the GVV methodology (Gentile, 2017).

To develop a high-quality online training program, the organization should request the assistance of technology experts (e.g., IT support). These technology experts can ensure that the training program operates effectively while minimizing the potential for program glitches before, during, and after training administration. Lastly, the organization should design the training program with trainee needs in mind. In particular, online training programs should be designed such that learning objectives are met, and trainees are given control over program features such as exercises, quizzes, and additional information (Antes, 2014; Landers & Reddock, 2017). To develop an online training program that can meet learning objectives and offer control to trainees, the organization should seek the assistance of experts trained in instructional design.

Many options exist when it comes to online training programs. In addition to the adoption of the delivery methods discussed in the face-to-face delivery methods section, ethics training managers can incorporate presentation slides, simulations, games, virtual reality components, quizzes, or intelligent tutoring systems, among other potential options. In considering these potential options, it is important to bear in mind the purpose of the training and not get distracted by the flashiness of novel technology features.

All of these delivery methods may offer potential benefits to trainees just as any face-to-face delivery method can prove beneficial. For example, simulations, games, or virtual reality can immerse trainees in realistic ethical scenarios and allow them to practice responding to ethical issues without real-world consequences. Quizzes or intelligent tutoring systems, on the other hand, allow trainees to engage with the material by guessing what the correct answer may be and learning as they receive feedback from the system. Regardless of the decision on the specific online delivery method or methods used, trainees should be able to navigate the training program, and meeting the instructional objectives should be a priority.

Blended/hybrid instructional approach

At the intersection of face-to-face and online training exists a third delivery approach—blended learning. Blended, or hybrid, learning combines elements of face-to-face and online training (Garrison & Kanuka, 2004). In a meta-analysis comparing face-to-face, online, and blended approaches to ethics training, it was found that blended approaches yielded the strongest effects on trainee learning, with purely online approaches showing the weakest effects (Todd, Watts et al., 2017). It appears that blended approaches may allow ethics training managers to leverage the unique benefits of both face-to-face and online formats. For example, awareness-based content can often be effectively delivered online while analysis- or action-based content is more effectively delivered in a face-to-face format. Trainees can learn about basic legal issues and organizational policies at their own pace online prior to applying this content in face-to-face exercises such as role plays and case discussions. To minimize confusion, ethics training managers adopting a hybrid approach should ensure there is a smooth transition between online and face-to-face components of the training. The content presented in each delivery format should complement the other to maximize overall training impact.

Steps for selecting and implementing delivery methods

The selection and implementation of delivery methods is only as effective as the principles and rationale behind those decisions (Salas, Tannenbaum, Kraiger, & Smith-Jentsch, 2012). A series of steps should be followed to effectively select and implement delivery methods into any training program. The figure presented in Chapter 4 provides a useful overview for understanding how delivery methods fit into the training program as a whole. Prior to selecting delivery methods, it is critical to specify learning objectives (Chapter 5), select evaluation methods (Chapter 6), and identify relevant training content (Chapter 7). Once these activities have been completed, the ethics training manager must now make a series of decisions, as described in the following sections, surrounding the delivery methods to be implemented in the training program.

Matching training content with delivery methods

The delivery methods reviewed in this chapter all have advantages and disadvantages. For example, some techniques are more effective at delivering large amounts of information to trainees in a short period of time (e.g., lecture, PowerPoint slides) while others are more effective at building complex skills (e.g., role play, case discussion) (Mulhearn et al., 2017). As such, the training content should be matched with the appropriate instructional technique to maximize learning potential.

Figure 8.1 offers a framework for matching ethics training content with delivery methods. The area above the double-headed arrow shows various delivery methods that range from passive to active. Passive delivery

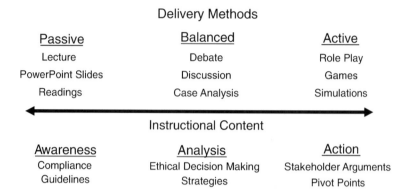

Figure 8.1 Framework for Matching Instructional Content with Delivery Methods.

methods like lecture, PowerPoint slides, and readings tend to involve one-way communication (i.e., trainer to trainee). In contrast, active delivery methods like role plays, games, and simulations, tend to support more active interactions, including two-way interactions between the trainer and trainees and interactions among trainees. Balanced delivery methods, which fall in the middle of the spectrum, include debate, discussion, and case analysis. In the area below the double-headed arrows, three major types of instructional content are presented (see Chapter 7), including awareness, analysis, and action.

Figure 8.1 is intended to serve as a guide for matching training content with delivery methods. Greater benefits of training content are expected when this content is delivered using complementary methods. For example, passive delivery methods are ideal for communicating awareness-based content. Balanced delivery methods may also be appropriate for awareness-based content, but active delivery methods are likely least useful. In contrast, active methods are ideal for delivering action-based content, while they are not especially useful for awareness content. Finally, balanced methods may be ideal for delivering analysis-based content.

Of course, there are exceptions and contingencies inherent in each type of content or delivery method used in ethics training. However, this framework should serve to illustrate that certain delivery methods are often better suited for certain types of instructional content. Also, it should be noted that selecting delivery methods typically boils down to *what combination* of delivery methods to use rather than deciding on just one to use throughout the training program.

Sequencing content

Not only must the training content be matched appropriately with delivery methods, this content must also be sequenced logically. Foundational concepts should be covered before asking trainees to engage with and apply these concepts (Anderson, 1996). For instance, it may be important to lecture on privacy and confidentiality issues prior to asking trainees to read and respond to a case that involves responding to privacy and confidentiality concerns. This sequence of learning from basic to more complex skills can be best illustrated by Kolb's (1976) four-stage model of learning. These four stages involve concrete experience, reflective observation, abstract conceptualization, and active experimentation. As illustrated by this classic model, learning begins with concrete, simple material and progressively moves toward more abstract and complex material, which may come in the form of cases or role plays.

Make it active

For trainees to learn a complex skill such as ethical decision making, they cannot sit idly by as trainers lecture on the topic ad nauseum. Instead, trainees must actively engage with the material to facilitate better understanding and long-term retention (Todd, Torrence, et al., 2017). Two key aspects of training are important in this regard: practice and feedback. Practice allows trainees the opportunity to produce a desired response that is tied to the learning objectives. Practice can take place in-person, through role play or case discussion, or online, through simulations, games, or web-based discussion. Regardless of the practice activities used, trainees should be given multiple opportunities to practice applying and using the training material.

The benefits of practice can be enhanced when coupled with feedback provided by the trainer. Feedback provides information about how the trainee is performing compared to an acceptable level of performance. For example, if a trainee provides an ineffective response to a case, the trainer can provide feedback about alternative solutions that may be more effective.

Feedback, like practice, can be incorporated into both face-to-face and on-line training programs. Regardless of whether the feedback comes from the trainer or a standardized computer program, the feedback should be directed toward the trainee's behavior rather than the trainee as an individual. Overall, practice and feedback can be thought of as the glue and tape that help the content learned in training programs to 'stick' (Goldstein & Ford, 2002). Without these two adhesive properties, any new concepts or skills learned in training will likely 'fall apart' before transferring back to trainees' jobs.

Make it meaningful

In addition to making the training active, trainees are more likely to learn and retain information when the training is meaningful to them personally and professionally (Fudge & Schlacter, 1999). On the surface, this may appear difficult in the case of ethics given that handling ethical problems is unlikely to be directly listed on any job description. However, showing that ethical concerns cut across all jobs and can have massive financial and strategic implications for the organization can help foster a training program that is meaningful for all trainees.

Aside from demonstrating that ethics matters, ethics training managers should also incorporate training content and practice activities that can be applied immediately following training (see Chapter 9). This can be done by providing trainees with helpful hints for becoming more aware of ethical concerns in their daily work. For example, trainees can be trained to think more deliberately about filling out an expense report to properly account for expenditures. To provide another example, trainees can be asked to consider the ethical implications of the tactics commonly used to solicit new business. Further, role play scenarios based on real organizational examples can show trainees a direct link to real-life organizational concerns. In addition to providing practical organizational examples to trainees, trainees can be asked to reflect on how they can apply training principles to their specific job tasks.

Selecting trainers

One final key decision to be made when implementing delivery methods involving face-to-face components is the selection of appropriate trainers.

Indeed, the individual, or individuals, who deliver the training material can also greatly impact the effectiveness of the program. Several features are generally associated with more effective trainers. For example, the most effective trainers tend to be well-organized, knowledgeable, enthusiastic about the subject matter, and capable of making clear connections among training concepts (Bartlett, 1982). Recent evidence suggests that using multiple highly skilled trainers in the same session can also greatly improve the effectiveness of ethics training programs (Watts et al., 2017). In other words, ethics trainers should not only be skilled instructors, they should also be knowledgeable about the principles of ethical decision making and the unique ethical issues that are most relevant to trainees. In a similar vein, trainers should also be familiar with organizational processes to make clear connections to relevant workplace scenarios that employees may actually encounter. An obvious disconnect between the content presented by the trainer and workplace realities will undoubtedly demotivate trainees.

Conclusion

Imagine two training programs—let's call them program A and program B. Training program A is equipped with the latest technology and contains all of the bells and whistles that trainees expect to see in today's digital world. After implementation, however, you discover that trainees are not learning much from program A and that the trainees find it to be confusing and cumbersome. On the other hand, training program B incorporates multiple instructional approaches as well as practice and feedback. Content in program B is primarily delivered face-to-face with some supplementary online materials to reinforce learning. Evaluation of program B suggests that trainees find the training to be engaging and they are improving at solving ethical problems in their work.

These two hypothetical training programs illustrate a common dilemma faced by ethics training managers. With recent innovations such as augmented reality, virtual reality, smartphones, and tablets, managers may feel compelled to develop a fun, flashy training program to attract—and keep—the attention of trainees. Unfortunately, such flashy techniques do not guarantee learning, and in some instances may compromise learning while increasing training costs. Returning to the analogy of delivery methods as vehicles for transporting cargo, different vehicles have different functions. Sports cars can, of course, be used to deliver cargo, but other less flashy modes of transportation may provide more effective, cost-efficient, and reliable transportation options. In other words, when selecting a vehicle for training content, managers should always keep in mind the purpose of ethics training—to facilitate trainee learning and skill acquisition.

References

Anderson, J. R. (1996). ACT: A simple theory of complex cognition. *American Psychologist, 51,* 355.

Antes, A. L., Murphy, S. T., Waples, E. P., Mumford, M. D., Brown, R. P., Connelly, S., & Devenport, L. D. (2009). A meta-analysis of ethics instruction effectiveness in the sciences. *Ethics & Behavior, 19,* 379–402.

Antes, A. L. (2014). A systematic approach to instruction in research ethics. *Accountability in Research, 21,* 50–67.

Bagdasarov, Z., MacDougall, A. E., Johnson, J. F., & Mumford, M. D. (2015). In case you didn't know: Recommendations for case-based ethics training. *Business law and ethics: Concepts, methodologies, tools, and applications.* (pp. 1480–1505). Hershey, PA: IGI Global.

Bartlett, C. J. (1982). *Teaching scale developed for Division of Behavioral and Social Sciences.* College Park, MD: University of Maryland.

Brown, L., Murphy, E., & Wade, V. (2006). Corporate eLearning: Human resource development implications for large and small organizations. *Human Resource Development International, 9,* 415–427.

Brummel, B. J., Gunsalus, C. K., Anderson, K. L., & Loui, M. C. (2010). Development of role-play scenarios for teaching responsible conduct of research. *Science and Engineering Ethics, 16,* 573–589.

Clark, R. C., & Mayer, R. E. (2016). *E-Learning and the science of instruction: Proven guidelines for consumers and designers of multimedia learning* (4th ed.). Hoboken, NJ: Wiley.

Fudge, R. S., & Schlacter, J. L. (1999). Motivating employees to act ethically: An expectancy theory approach. *Journal of Business Ethics, 18,* 295–304.

Garrison, D. R., & Kanuka, H. (2004). Blended learning: Uncovering its transformative potential in higher education. *The Internet and Higher Education, 7,* 95–105.

Gentile, M. C. (2012). Values-driven leadership development: Where we have been and where we could go. *Organization Management Journal, 9,* 188–196.

Gentile, M. C. (2017). Giving voice to values: A pedagogy for behavioral ethics. *Journal of Management Education, 41*, 469–479.

Goldstein, I. L., & Ford, J. K. (2002). *Training in organizations* (4th ed.). Belmont, CA: Wadsworth Cengage Learning.

Kaddoura, M. (2013). Think pair share: A teaching learning strategy to enhance students' critical thinking. *Educational Research Quarterly, 36*, 3–24.

Kolb, D. A. (1976). Management and the learning process. *California Management Review, 18*, 21–31.

Landers, R. N., & Reddock, C. M. (2017). A meta-analytic investigation of objective learner control in web-based instruction. *Journal of Business and Psychology, 32*, 455–478.

Mencl, J., & May, D. R. (2009). The effects of proximity and empathy on ethical decision-making: An exploratory investigation. *Journal of Business Ethics, 85*, 201–226.

Mulhearn, T. J., Steele, L. M., Watts, L. L., Medeiros, K. E., Mumford, M. D., & Connelly, S. (2017). Review of instructional approaches in ethics education. *Science and Engineering Ethics, 23*, 883–912.

Noe, R. A. (2013). *Employee training and development.* New York, NY: McGraw Hill.

Salas, E., Tannenbaum, S. I., Kraiger, K., & Smith-Jentsch, K. A. (2012). The science of training and development in organizations: What matters in practice. *Psychological Science in the Public Interest, 13*, 74–101.

Todd, E. M., Torrence, B. S., Watts, L. L., Mulhearn, T. J., Connelly, S., & Mumford, M. D. (2017). Effective practices in the delivery of research ethics education: A qualitative review of instructional methods. *Accountability in Research, 24*, 297–321.

Todd, E. M., Watts, L. L., Mulhearn, T. J., Torrence, B. S., Turner, M. R., Connelly, S., & Mumford, M. D. (2017). A meta-analytic comparison of face-to-face and online delivery in ethics instruction: The case for a hybrid approach. *Science and Engineering Ethics, 23*, 1719–1754.

Watts, L. L., Medeiros, K. E., Mulhearn, T. J., Steele, L. M., Connelly, S., & Mumford, M. D. (2017). Are ethics training programs improving? A meta-analytic review of past and present ethics instruction in the sciences. *Ethics & Behavior, 27*, 351–384.

Weber, J., & Wasieleski, D. M. (2013). Corporate ethics and compliance programs: A report, analysis and critique. *Journal of Business Ethics, 112*, 609–626.

PART III

MAKING IT STICK

9

POST-TRAINING CARE

Kelsey E. Medeiros

***

Imagine for a moment that you've decided to purchase a new plant for your home. You drive to your nearest plant nursery and scour the grounds for the most beautiful greenery you can find. As you scan the outdoor garden center, you notice the perfect tree in the left, shaded corner. You find a pot that looks appealing and grab a large bag of plant fertilizer as you head to the counter to make your purchase. The cashier at the register mentions that this tree does best in a shaded environment and most definitely belongs outdoors. Ignoring the advice of the cashier, you return home, plant your new tree in the pot, and set it in the sunniest corner of your bedroom where you will see it every morning when you wake up.

Your new morning routine involves waking up at sunrise, turning to your plant, and chanting 'grow, grow, grow!' After 2 weeks, you notice that your plant is not growing. Sure, you haven't watered it, researched how to properly care for it, or even put it in a location where it would thrive. But that shouldn't matter—you've been telling it to grow! In disbelief, you give up on your morning ritual and allow your once beautiful plant to wither away in the corner. You conclude that something was clearly wrong with that plant.

The idea that chanting to a plant will spur growth without considering any additional care likely sounds absurd. It is. Most of us would laugh at someone who approached plant care in this fashion. What is striking, however, is the similarity between this scenario and the approach most organizations take to their post-ethics training efforts. If you substitute the plant with a well-developed training effort, and 'grow, grow, grow' with 'be ethical,' you've just read the typical post-training approach to ethics trainings.

Failure to account for factors that facilitate the application of ethics training content and employee ethical growth outside of training will likely lead to limited, if any, real change for even the most well-designed training efforts. Much like the plant, employees' ethical skills will be left to wither away without the necessary guidance and appropriate environmental conditions to thrive. If organizations want their ethics training initiatives to have a lasting impact, it is critical to understand how to best facilitate employee ethical growth outside of the immediate training environment. As such, this chapter aims to provide practical suggestions for professionals looking to maximize training effectiveness by addressing the following question: What is the necessary environment and post-training care to ensure that employees apply what they have learned to ethically thrive?

Why the post-training environment matters

The idea that the post-training environment plays an important role in the application of training content to the workplace was recognized by scholars and practitioners in the 1980s. Scholars were interested in what became known as the 'transfer problem,' or the failure to apply newly learned skills and knowledge to the work environment (Baldwin & Ford, 1988). At the time, organizations were siphoning money into expensive, elaborate training programs that simply were not producing results. Early reports estimated that only 10% of skills and knowledge learned during training were transferred to the work environment (Georgenson, 1982). Others, more recently, have estimated that initial transfer rates are closer to 50%, indicating approximately half of those completing a training program apply the content to their day-to-day work. This number declines to approximately 30%, however, when looking at long-term application, suggesting that close to 70% of employees are not applying training content within 1 year of completing the training program (Saks, 2002). Put differently, some employees may be using what they have learned outside of the training environment immediately following training, but very few are sustaining this application over a long period of time. Much of this is likely due to a failure to consider how the organizational infrastructure can help support application and continued learning. When the post-training environment is not considered, long-term behavioral change does not occur and, ultimately, an organization wastes its money on a fruitless effort.

Unfortunately, little is known about the transfer of ethics-specific training content to the workplace. The information that is available, however, is not promising. For example, researchers at the University of Oklahoma conducted a review of business-focused ethics trainings to assess their effectiveness (Medeiros et al., 2017). They reviewed over 40 studies that empirically evaluated the effectiveness of ethics training courses delivered to business students and professionals. Across the included studies, ethics trainings had a small to moderate influence. A few studies that were included in the review also explored the long-term impact of training. For these studies, this influence declined over time revealing a near zero impact of ethics training efforts in the long term. Critically, however, very few of the included studies examined the long-term impact of training. In fact, only four studies did so. From a scientific perspective, more research is needed to fully understand when and how these trainings may have a long-term impact.

Those four studies do shed some light, however, on the potential lasting effects of ethics training programs. For instance, Lordanis Kavathatzopoulos (Kavathatzopoulos, 1994) at Uppsala University in Sweden looked at the impact of an ethics training aimed at improving problem-solving skills in a group of 17 managers working at a Swedish pharmaceutical company. The researcher asked the managers to respond to a series of ethical scenarios prior to the training, immediately following the training, and again 1 month following the training. Scores improved significantly from before to after the training and remained moderately stable 1 month following the training. However, the scores after 1 month of training did begin to slightly decline, though they were still much higher than scores at the beginning of training and similar to those immediately following training.

In another example, Jonathon Halbesleben and colleagues examined the immediate and long-term effects of an ethics training program (Halbesleben, Wheeler, & Buckley, 2005). The researchers provided the training to an undergraduate Principles of Management class and compared the results to an undergraduate Human Resource Management class who did not receive any ethics training. They asked the students to estimate how likely they believed they were to commit an unethical act at school as well as in a business setting prior to the training, immediately following the training, and at the end of the semester. Those who received the ethics training stated that they would be less likely to engage in unethical behavior in a business setting immediately following the training and again at the end of the semester. The estimate made at the end of the semester, however, was similar to the estimate noted immediately following the training. Despite somewhat promising results, it is important to note that the researchers only examined *perceived* future behavior rather than *actual* behavior. As such, this study says little about how someone will actually act and more about how they think they will act.

Results from these studies are hopeful in that those who received ethics training did not revert back to pre-training attitudes or responses. In fact, there was no statistically significant difference between results immediately following training and those measured at a later time point. In other words, from a statistical perspective, there was no change. However, it is important to again emphasize that there are too few studies on the long-term impacts of ethics training to draw any meaningful conclusions. Additionally, the two studies mentioned looked at the effects of ethics training after 1 month and a few weeks, respectively. How long a change like this actually lasts remains a key question. Many of these studies also do not consider what role environmental characteristics play in helping to sustain or continue to improve results obtained immediately after training and what the effect is on ethical behavior in the workplace.

Although one interpretation of these results suggests that organizations should simply give up because ethics training may be wasting organizational resources, an alternative explanation may be that few organizations consider how ethics training programs align with the broader organizational context and what steps they must take to facilitate the transfer of ethics training content to the work environment. The effectiveness of an ethics training program depends heavily on the application of learned skills and knowledge to the everyday work environment. Organizations can facilitate this process by creating what scholars refer to as a transfer climate (Burke & Baldwin, 1999). A transfer climate is a component of the larger organizational climate that encourages employees to apply what they have learned in training to their job—the ultimate goal of ethics training efforts. Transfer climates have several components but empirical research supports the strong influence of particular environmental factors including leader support, systems alignment, peer influence, and practice opportunities (Blume, Ford, Baldwin, & Huang, 2010; Burke & Hutchins, 2007).

Figure 9.1 provides an overview of these components, highlighting that training itself, although the central focus, makes up only a small portion of the organizational environment that influences ethical behavior. Instead, each component that will be discussed sits as part of the broader organizational system with each layer radiating out to create an ethically supportive organizational system.

Organizational systems

As noted in Chapter 1, many equate compliance with ethics. If an organization has the right policies and procedures in place, they believe that

Ethics training

Post-training practice

Peer support

Leader support

Organizational systems

Figure 9.1 Influence of Post-training Environment on Ethics Training Application.

their employees will behave ethically, or at a minimum that they will be legally protected if their employees break the law. However, as discussed previously, there are plenty of case examples to suggest that ethics-focused policies are simply not enough. Although policies may prove ineffective on their own, they can support an ethical environment and reinforce the content and values communicated in training. Well-designed policies that facilitate the application of training material allow employees to appropriately apply what they have learned. For instance, ethics trainings regularly include a component focused on organizational policies related to reporting ethical violations. Simply communicating the policy is not enough, however, if the underlying culture does not support such reporting. Take the following case as an example.

Case 9.1   Susie's Policy Problems

Susie is a new hire at a medium-sized consulting firm and has recently finished her mandatory, 1-day, ethics training seminar. In the seminar, the trainers discussed the importance of reporting ethical violations and the mechanism by which to report them, including calling the ethics hotline and discussing the issue with a direct supervisor. Within her first month on the job, Susie witnesses one of her peers padding their consulting budget for a project—a practice that was strictly discouraged in ethics training. She asks her coworker who says, 'it's no big deal—everyone does it.' Still feeling uncomfortable with the situation, she consults the employee handbook she was given on her first day but cannot find any specific information about whether or not this is allowed. Susie then speaks to her manager, noting that she believes someone on her team is behaving unethically and wanted to raise the issue. Her manager, Jill, states that 'it happens from time to time, and there's really no need to report it any further.' Susie still feels that something is not right. She decides to call the company's anonymous ethics hotline, which was an alternative step described in the ethics training. When she does so, she is greeted by an answering machine which directs her to leave a message. She leaves a message describing the incident. One month later, nothing has been done about the issue. Susie begins to think, maybe this behavior is okay after all, and that next time she witnesses something like this, she won't waste her time trying to report it.

In Susie's case, the training clearly communicated expectations to her, but the environment failed to support and encourage the application of the reporting practices described. In this instance, the environment is likely to win out over the formal training as more and more environmental cues will suggest that, despite what she was told in training, this behavior is actually acceptable. In contrast, the following example demonstrates how systems can be aligned to support new ethical knowledge and skills.

Case 9.2   Bobby the Bully

Steve is beginning his first job at Tech Inc., a growing tech firm based in California. In his first week, Steve attends a typical set of new employee orientations, including a session on ethics and compliance. A common theme across all of the sessions was that Tech Inc. has currently undergone a cultural transformation. They previously faced issues with bullying and are trying to rid their culture of such negative behavior. 'We are taking this issue seriously,' says a senior leader during one of the orientations. During his second week at work, however, his new teammates start asking him to fetch coffee and run their errands during work time. As the new guy, Steve follows their instructions thinking that he wants to get along with everyone. The requests continue into his third and fourth weeks and seem to be getting more extreme. One of his coworkers, Bobby, keeps asking him to do particularly inappropriate tasks such as making copies of his child's birthday party invitations on the office copier. When Steve tells Bobby that he doesn't feel comfortable using office resources in that way, the teammate simply said, 'What, are you scared or something?' He then called the attention of his other teammates saying, 'Guys! Steve is scared of the copy machine.' They all break out in laughter and start taunting him with profane nicknames. Steve leaves work that day feeling deflated. What a terrible place to work, he thinks. When he gets home, he consults the company's ethics policy handbook, which states that the company has a zero tolerance policy for bullying and that the behavior should be immediately reported to HR. The next morning, Steve composes an email to HR outlining the facts of what had happened over the past few weeks. Within 2 days, the issue was being investigated, during which evidence surfaced of multiple other instances of Bobby bullying new employees. Despite being a top performer, Bobby was fired later that week. The other team members were spoken to and later apologized to Steve.

In Steve's case, the importance of the issue is communicated via senior management, there are policies in place to support ridding the company of this negative behavior, and the company followed through on their policy. In other words, the organizational systems were aligned to discourage the inappropriate behavior. For Steve, this will reinforce what he learned in training and reaffirm the organization's commitment to the issue. Further, others in the team will likely be dissuaded from engaging in such behavior. In comparison to Susie's case, Steve's case provides us with an example of how system alignment can work to manage behavior effectively.

Leadership

As seen in the previous examples, leaders play a pivotal role in setting the post-training tone by communicating the organization's values and emphasizing the importance of ethical practices. In her pioneering work on ethical leadership, Linda Trevino, a Professor at Smeal College of Business at Penn State University, and her colleagues describe two key components—the moral person and the moral manager (Trevino, Hartman, & Brown, 2000). The moral person refers to the ethicality and integrity of the ethical leader. In other words, does the leader possess ethical values, integrity, and ethicality? The moral manager refers to a leader's responsibility to encourage ethical behavior in his or her followers. This is accomplished through many mechanisms including communicating expectations and standards, rewarding and punishing behavior, and role modeling ethical behavior. All three are critical to helping employees transfer the content they learn in training to their everyday work environment.

The first way in which leaders impact the post-training environment is by bolstering what their employees learned in training. This is most commonly accomplished by communicating the importance and value of training, emphasizing the application of training content to the work environment, and regularly discussing the training content (Burke & Hutchins, 2007). By engaging in these activities, a leader underscores the importance of training to the employee and signals that the leader values ethical behavior. Regular discussions should be held around ethical practices in the team and organization, as well as expectations regarding how to handle ethical issues. Further, leaders may consider emphasizing an 'open door' policy in which employees are encouraged to bring ethical issues to their leader. It logically follows, that ethical leaders must then also be good listeners, giving voice to their employees by encouraging them to speak up about ethical issues they face in the workplace and helping them, when needed, work through the appropriate steps to make a decision and act.

Another way in which leaders reinforce training content is by role modeling the appropriate behavior. Have you ever heard a leader say, 'Do as I say, not as I do?' This attitude tends to be ineffective for encouraging and facilitating appropriate behavior, especially when it comes to ethics. A leader's behavior speaks far louder than his or her words, as a leader's behavior signals the true values to followers. Take for example a leader who says he or she values honesty. However, this leader is known for lying to followers and peers in order to reach a goal. The leader's action of lying suggests to followers that statements about valuing honesty may be empty and that the leader may prefer a lie or a fib if it helps get the job done. Although no leader should expect to be perfect all the time, it is imperative to display ethical behavior and the highest of ethical standards for employees. Specific to training transfer, by displaying the behaviors learned in training, the leader reinforces that these behaviors are expected in this work environment. Conversely, if a leader does not role model ethical behavior, it signals that what the employees learned in training is not how it is actually done in practice and that training can be disregarded. Again, a leader's behavior can severely undermine a training effort and, thus, must be carefully crafted to align with the training content if it is to encourage the learned behavior.

Although the goal of any ethics training should center around preventing unethical behavior by encouraging ethical decision making, leaders may still have to respond retroactively to unethical behavior. A leader's action in these moments may further enforce or, alternatively, degrade the information communicated in training. In this sense, leaders must follow through on what it is they say they will do and commit to enforcing the policies that they encourage. One way in which leaders do this is by rewarding ethical behavior and punishing unethical behavior. Specifically, if an issue is brought to the attention of the leader, he or she must follow the proper investigative procedures and respond accordingly. It is important to note here that this can often be challenging for leaders. When a report is brought to their attention, they must not jump to conclusions and immediately take a side. Instead, they must hear the perspectives of all parties, collect the relevant evidence, and then make a conclusion regarding the suggested infraction based on the body of evidence available. However, if an employee is found to have behaved unethically, that employee should be appropriately punished in a timely manner. By doing so, this sends a signal to other employees that this behavior is unacceptable. This can be particularly impactful for followers when the unethical behavior is committed by a high performer. Conversely, if the leader does not punish this behavior, it would signal to employees that this behavior is something that they can get away with, thereby undermining what they learned in training.

Peers

Like leaders, peers are critical to supporting training efforts (Martin, 2010). Peers reinforce training efforts by demonstrating behavior aligned with the training content and by encouraging the application of content to the new work environment. While a leader's influence stems from an authoritative or power-based relationship in which he or she does not observe a follower's behavior regularly and consistently, a peer is on the front lines. Peers have such a large influence on trainees due to their proximity and frequency of contact with one another. They simply have more contact and interaction than a leader.

The role of peers in facilitating transfer is based on social learning theory, which argues that, while some of our learning comes from direct experience (e.g., training), a large portion of how we learn stems from observations of others (Bandura, 1971). In a transfer context, employees continue to learn after leaving training by observing their peers' behavior. As such, how peers behave also signals to others what behavior is acceptable and not acceptable in their specific working environment. If a trainee leaves ethics training with the right attitude and essential skills for handling ethical issues, but their peers suggest that 'this isn't the way it is done around here,' the effectiveness of training content faces a high chance of being lost over time.

Practice

In addition to support from peers, a transfer climate is also characterized by additional opportunities to perform the newly learned knowledge and skills on-the-job, which allows employees to sustain and improve their learning after leaving the initial training environment (Clarke, 2002). Employees will inevitably face ethical dilemmas in the workplace after training and will then organically have the opportunity to apply what they've learned. However, organizations can also facilitate these opportunities by providing planned practice. Just as practice opportunities during the training allow employees to apply their newly learned skills and knowledge in a safe environment in which feedback is provided, so do post-training activities. Providing employees with new cases, role-plays, and discussion opportunities extends the learning environment outside of the immediate training context and encourages the continued application of training material in the work environment. These practice opportunities should be facilitated in some manner and involve critical feedback. The importance of feedback in the training context has been discussed in Chapter 8, and the same principles apply here. By coupling post-training practice with feedback, employees receive critical insight on their performance or application of training material in a safe environment, rather than feedback after making a critical error in an ethical dilemma on the job.

The importance of feedback also suggests that those providing the feedback must be trained and prepared to do so effectively. How these practice opportunities take form and who provides the feedback then becomes a critical question. There are multiple ways in which this can be accomplished. Perhaps the most efficient way for delivering post-training practice is through online modules which provide automatic feedback to employees. As noted in Chapter 8, while it may be easy for organizations to deploy such online practice tools, they may not provide meaningful practice opportunities which result in real results. Instead, if companies want to take advantage of the online learning environment, it may be more useful to combine an online module with in-person practice opportunities. In-person practice could be delivered through follow-up training sessions that complement the primary training, facilitation guides for managers which provide short activities that can be accomplished during weekly meetings, or follow-up team or one-on-one discussions after completion of an online training module. The in-person portion can be facilitated by managers, trainers, or peer leaders. Other options include novel online approaches such as social cohort-based learning models. As highlighted in Chapter 8, however, whoever is chosen to lead or facilitate these efforts should be fully invested in the importance of training and communicating its value in order to encourage genuine investment and engagement in the practice opportunities.

Preparing the post-training environment

To best prepare the environment, it is first critical that leaders have a clear understanding of the current environment. In fact, although the present chapter is focused on *post* training, understanding the *pre*-training environment provides insight on what needs to change but also the attitudes and practices shaping current beliefs, which can impact the effectiveness of training itself. Understanding the environment can most effectively be accomplished during the organizational, environmental, and stakeholder analyses described in Chapter 5. In addition to collecting information on readiness and resources, this analysis may also collect information about leader attitudes toward the training and ethics efforts, perceptions of existing policies, as well as common departmental, team, or organizational practices related to ethics. Based on results from this analysis, leaders can then identify existing practices and attitudes that will support the training effort and those that may challenge it. Those identified as potential challenges should be addressed prior to training.

When considering the environment, there are several guiding questions that may help identify areas that will support, and those that may challenge, the transfer of training. Below are questions that may help guide these efforts. It is important to note that this list is not exhaustive, nor is it meant to be rigidly applied to every organization. Rather, these questions should be viewed as guides that can help leaders consider organizational factors that may impact training.

- Do our employees believe being ethical is important to our company?
- Do our employees believe ethics training is valuable?
- Do our organizational policies encourage ethical practices?

- Do our organizational leaders encourage ethical practices in our company?
- Do our organizational leaders believe ethics training is valuable?
- How can we provide our employees with opportunities to practice once they have left training?

Conclusion

Although the training environment is often a key focus when it comes to designing effective training efforts, as this chapter has hopefully demonstrated, a focus on the immediate training environment alone is not enough. Attention must also be paid to the post-training environment if ethics training programs are to prove effective. The ethical attitudes, values, and decision-making skills learned during training must be reinforced through continued practice and a supportive environment to ensure that they do not wither away with time. Organizations must align broader organizational systems and climate to support the training effort in order to see any real change in the ethical behavior and decision making of its employees. Investment in ethics training, then, requires more than effective training design—it requires a careful consideration, alignment, and care of organizational characteristics that will allow ethical behavior, decision making, and values to flourish.

References

Baldwin, T. T., & Ford, J. K. (1988). Transfer of training: A review and directions for future research. *Personnel Psychology, 41*, 63–105.

Bandura, A. (1971). *Social learning theory*. New York, NY: General Learning Corporation.

Blume, B. D., Ford, J. K., Baldwin, T. T., & Huang, J. L. (2010). Transfer of training: A meta-analytic review. *Journal of Management, 36*, 1065–1105.

Burke, L. A., & Baldwin, T. T. (1999). Workforce training transfer: A study of the effect of relapse prevention training and transfer climate. *Human Resource Management, 38*(3), 227–242.

Burke, L. A., & Hutchins, H. M. (2007). Training transfer: An integrative literature review. *Human Resource Development Review, 6*(3), 263–296.

Clarke, N. (2002). Job/work environment factors influencing training effectiveness within a human service agency: Some indicative support for

Baldwin and Ford's transfer climate construct. *International Journal of Training and Development, 6,* 146–162.

Georgenson, D. L. (1982). The problem of transfer calls for partnership. *Training and Development Journal, 36,* 75–78.

Halbesleben, J. R. B., Wheeler, A. R., & Buckley, M. R. (2005). Everybody else is doing it, so why can't we? Pluralistic ignorance and business ethics education. *Journal of Business Ethics, 56,* 385–398.

Kavathatzopoulos, I. (1994). Training professional managers in decision-making about real life business ethics problems: The acquisition of the autonomous problem-solving skill. *Journal of Business Ethics, 13,* 379–386.

Martin, H. J. (2010). Workplace climate and peer support as determinants of training transfer. *Human Resource Development Quarterly, 21*(1), 87–104.

Medeiros, K. E., Watts, L. L., Mulhearn, T. J., Steele, L. M., Mumford, M. D., & Connelly, S. (2017). What is working, what is not, and what we need to know: A meta-analytic review of business ethics education. *Journal of Academic Ethics, 15,* 245–275.

Saks, A. M. (2002). So what is a good transfer of training estimate? A reply to Fitzpatrick. *The Industrial-Organizational Psychologist, 39,* 29–30.

Trevino, L. K., Hartman, L. P., & Brown, M. (2000). Moral person and moral manager: How executives develop a reputation for ethical leadership. *California Management Review, 42,* 128–142.

10

PILOT TESTING AND IMPLEMENTATION

Kelsey E. Medeiros

***

You're trying to sell the product to regular people, but you didn't actually put it in the hands of regular people!—*Silicon Valley*, Season 3, Episode 9

For those who are unfamiliar with the television series, *Silicon Valley*, the show presents a look at the successes, but mostly struggles, of a start-up tech company. The series follows Richard Hendricks, the founder of Pied Piper, and his team as they develop, pitch, launch, pivot, and manage their innovative data storage network. In one episode, the team finds that their new platform is being downloaded rapidly, but that users are not actively and regularly using the platform. One member of the team, Monica, conducts focus groups to identify the issue and finds that everyone is 'totally freaked out' by the platform. It is then that she summarizes the problem to the team with this chapter's opening quote. The team never put the product in the hands of those who were going to use it and, in doing so, missed major flaws and issues that could have potentially been avoided (Tobias, 2016).

Although you may not be launching a new software any time soon, you may face many of the same challenges as the Pied Piper team when developing and implementing an ethics training program. The content and the presentation of ethics training material may appear clear and meaningful to the designers. However, what makes perfect sense to the training managers may not make sense to trainees. One way to check how training and content and delivery will be perceived and received, as well as to identify potential implementation issues, is pilot testing. Pilot testing is the means by which managers gather initial feedback and test the training material on a small group from the intended audience. It may be easy to dismiss this chapter as common sense, obvious, or even unnecessary. However, common sense does not always equate to common practice. The following sections provide examples of the importance of pilot testing, the steps involved in running a successful pilot test, and strategies for successful training implementation.

The importance of pilot testing

Pilot testing is a critical step in the training design process (van Teijlingen & Hundley, 2001). Different industries refer to the pilot testing process with unique terminology. Generally, however, the intent of a pilot test is to assess the feasibility of a planned large-scale effort using a small group of people (Thabane et al., 2010). In medical research, this process is typically referred to as a vanguard trial, with the purpose of assessing safety risks, study feasibility, and optimal doses, among other criteria (Tavel & Fosdick, 2001). In social science research, pilot testing typically involves administering the planned research procedures to a small sample to identify any potential issues in administration and to ensure that the experiment is working as intended. In tech fields, alpha testing refers to the initial trial of a product by technical experts who can detect bugs and other glitches. Beta testing follows and is conducted with potential users to determine product readiness and customer satisfaction (Freiler, 2019). Drawing on these examples, four critical reasons for conducting a pilot test for ethics training emerge:

- Identify administrative and other practical issues.
- Provide advance warning about what may go wrong.

- Assess trainee readiness.
- Consider if the training is working as expected.

First, conducting a pilot training illuminates potential administrative and logistical problems that can cause significant disruptions during broader implementation. Just as providing practice opportunities helps to ensure that training content 'sticks' (see Chapter 8), there are likely several moving parts of the training that also require practice on the part of ethics training managers. One of the basic, but often overlooked, challenges is ensuring that training content and delivery methods are appropriate given the space available. For example, if a slide deck is being used to present visuals during training, it is important to determine if these slides will be visible to all trainees. As another example, group activities and discussions can be challenging in rooms with traditional theater- or classroom-style seating. In such layouts, trainees are typically not facing one another and the room design does not facilitate communication among more than one or two trainees at a time. Other logistical considerations that frequently emerge in pilot training include access to equipment and technology, printed handouts, and room access, as well as ADA (Americans with Disabilities Act) accessibility. When feasible, it is an ideal strategy to pilot test ethics training programs in the same location and using the same resources that will be used in the actual training.

Second, there are some issues that may be unavoidable, and a pilot training may help managers to identify these issues and plan for them in advance. Despite best intentions, some activities, questions, or content may not be well received, or may be misinterpreted by trainees. For instance, a case may turn out to be irrelevant to certain trainee groups, or trainees may misinterpret a case because of the way it is written. Discussion questions may present similar challenges, such that they appear clear to the ethics training managers, but lack clarity for trainees. If content is put in the hands of the trainees before implementing it broadly, these issues may be identified and addressed up front. By solving content issues that emerge during pilot training, ethics training managers can minimize the number of larger headaches downstream. For example, we can attest from personal experience that it is far easier and more cost effective to adjust content before hundreds or thousands of copies of training materials have been made!

Third, as noted in Chapter 9, trainee and manager attitudes can have a large impact on training success. Thus, it is important to consider attitudes during initial testing phases. To assess what trainees think about the training, consider asking them to report their attitudes and reactions concerning each major section and activity of the pilot training. Of course, as highlighted in previous chapters, it is important to monitor these attitudes over time as well. When pilot testing a new training, it may be important to assess if trainees view the training as useful. If they do not, then ethics training managers may need to make adjustments to the training to make it more valuable to the trainees. Alternatively, ethics training managers could focus more effort on communicating why this training is important.

Fourth, assessing the impact of training during the initial pilot tests can offer insight into whether or not the training is working in the intended manner. Asking pilot trainees to complete pre- and post-assessments may reveal important patterns regarding the effects of training (see Chapter 6). Depending on how many people are included in the pilot training, evaluations can be conducted formally or informally. Researchers generally recommend testing a minimum of 30 trainees to detect if the training resulted in meaningful changes in trainee knowledge or skills. At a minimum, managers can investigate if scores are trending in the expected direction. For example, managers might want to determine if knowledge scores have increased between pre- and post-test for those who complete the pilot training. If scores are not trending in the expected direction, this can signal to managers that certain aspects of the training should be refined.

How to conduct a pilot test

In line with alpha and beta testing in the tech industry, pilot testing an ethics training program should include two phases. The first phase focuses on expert review by ethics and training experts who can identify issues with the content and delivery methods. The second phase, similar to the beta test, asks for feedback from a small subset of trainees. The following sections provide an overview of how to conduct each phase. An overview of the process is provided in Figure 10.1.

Figure 10.1 Overview of the Pilot Training Process.

Phase 1

Phase 1 aims to provide training designers with feedback from experts outside of the design team. People innately have a preference for their own ideas (Onarheim & Christensen, 2012), so it is important to seek input from others who may be able to appraise these idea more objectively. When available, experts should include both applied ethics and training experts, as they will provide unique feedback regarding the proposed ethics training. Specifically, ethics experts can share insight on the accuracy and appropriateness of the content. In contrast, training experts will share feedback on improving the delivery of the training such as different activities or methods for delivering content. Experts can come from both within or outside of the organization, but it is important that experts are familiar enough with the field and industry to judge what ethical issues are most critical to incorporate in training. Examples of key groups to consult throughout the training design and pilot testing process include compliance, human resources, and legal departments. Depending on the organization, other stakeholders such as senior management or union leaders may also need to be involved at this point.

There is flexibility in how managers request this feedback, ranging from a brief survey to focus groups to interviews. Experts may even participate in the pilot training and provide feedback throughout or at the conclusion of the practice session. Which option to choose will depend on organizational and project constraints (e.g., time, personnel resources). However, it is highly recommended that managers elect for the option that will allow for the most amount of quality feedback given the existing constraints.

Ideally, training managers will seek feedback and input from experts throughout the design process. As such, it is recommended that experts be identified early on in the process and, when possible, be used as a resource throughout the design process. At a minimum, however, experts should be consulted once a minimum viable training product has been designed. In other words, experts should review the training material once an initial draft of the content and delivery methods has been finalized. Drafts of training activities and assessments, including instructions and materials, should also undergo expert review.

Once collected, the ethics training manager should review the expert feedback and consider which suggested changes can, and should, be incorporated into the training. Although expert advice should be carefully considered, it is not necessary, and sometimes not feasible, to make all the recommended changes. In addition to maximizing the effectiveness of training, it is also important to consider the time and feasibility constraints when deciding which changes to make. If necessary, after making the changes, training materials should be sent back out to the experts for another review. This process should be repeated until no additional major changes are recommended by the experts.

Phase 2

In phase 2, the pilot training is delivered to a small subset of trainees with the intent of identifying issues related to feasibility, practicality, administration, and initial evidence of effectiveness. This phase also acts as a practice opportunity for the trainers to rehearse on a small audience before rolling out the training to a larger group. Additionally, phase 2 aims to gauge the reactions and attitudes of the trainees, as well as the expected impact of the training. Trainees for the pilot training should be selected from the larger population of intended trainees. The sample should reflect the diversity and makeup of the trainee population to ensure that a representative sample of views and perspectives are incorporated into the initial assessment. For example, if trainees are to be selected from multiple locations, including trainees from each of these locations, or collecting a small pilot training in each location, allows for the identification of location-specific challenges.

The pilot training can be thought of as a final dress rehearsal—all the props are arranged and lines memorized. Or in restaurant terms, pilot training is like a soft-opening, in which guests are invited into a fully designed restaurant and are encouraged to provide feedback on the food while the staff perfects their service. As such, this phase of the process should ideally not be completed until all training materials are fully developed and have been finalized following expert review.

At this stage, trainers should also be asked to provide feedback on issues they faced while delivering the training. This can be accomplished through one-on-one meetings, surveys, or focus groups, depending on the number of trainers involved. Trainees should also, of course, provide their reactions to the training. As noted previously, while it is important to collect overall reactions, this phase may also include reactions to specific sections of training as well as activities or content. Additionally, reactions regarding the trainers, training room, and perceived relevance to the job or work environment may also be gathered. Collecting this specific information helps training managers to identify what exactly the trainees liked or disliked. If trainees simply provide a number representing their gut reaction to the training as a whole, managers will be hard pressed to know where to make changes.

Phase 2 also offers the benefit of providing insight on whether the training is producing the expected results. Just as described in the evaluation chapter (Chapter 6), trainees in the pilot training should complete the evaluation measures that will be used to assess training effectiveness. By doing so, managers can assess if the scores are trending in the expected direction. In other words, are trainees demonstrating that the learning objectives of training have been met? If yes, then the training is working appropriately. If no, then managers should use the available information to identify what it is about the training, or the transfer environment (see Chapter 9), that is failing to support change. At this stage, focus groups may be needed if the causes of these issues are not readily apparent.

As noted with regard to phase 1, phase 2 should be repeated with new groups of trainees as long as major changes are being made. This allows managers to evaluate the impacts of each major change. A summary of the pilot testing phases is provided in Table 10.1.

Strategies for successful training implementation

After completing the pilot testing and making the appropriate changes, ethics training managers will be ready for phase 3—training implementation and monitoring. At this point, the training should be well rehearsed and any expected bumps should have been ironed out. Still, new issues can arise during the implementation phase, which is why it is important to continuously monitor training efforts (discussed in more detail in Chapter 11). In addition to monitoring, there are several steps managers

Table 10.1 Pilot Testing Summary

	Phase 1: Expert Review	*Phase 2: Trainee Pilot and Review*
Who	Ethics and training experts	Sample of intended trainees
What	Review the content for accuracy and potential issues	Complete the training and provide feedback on content, activities, and administration
Where	Virtual or in-person	In the planned training environment
When	After initial content and activity development	After revisions from phase 1 and training is nearly finalized
Why	Catch potential errors and issues	Test feasibility, identify issues, gauge reactions, assess impact

Note. Each phase may be completed more than once. If significant changes are made after either phase, the phase should be repeated to pilot test the training with the changes.

can take to ensure a smooth training implementation. These steps include communicating early, designing an effective train-the-trainer program, scheduling, discussing positive results, investigating negative results, and planning for the unexpected.

Communicate early

How and when to best communicate about ethics training in an organization has not been directly researched. However, broader research on communicating training in organizations can provide some insight on best practices for ethics training. How and when the training is discussed in an organization can influence trainee motivation, a critical factor that supports trainee learning (Noe, 1986). One study found that how training efforts are framed can have an impact on employee motivation and actions (Quinones, 1995). However, although this study found that training labeled as 'remedial' resulted in the most learning by trainees, as compared to a 'specialized' or 'advanced' training, the same results may not be seen with ethics training. Findings suggest that people tend to view themselves as more ethical than the average person (Krueger, 1998), so the labeling and framing of ethics training may require special care. For example, framing ethics training as an opportunity to improve professional decision-making skills will likely be viewed as more motivating to trainees than the traditional framing of compliance training. This framing casts ethics training as a positive rather than a negative. Communicating this message and garnering excitement for the training early may help build enthusiasm and motivation which, in turn, can impact the effectiveness of the training session. Additionally, communicating the value of ethics training as a useful activity for trainee's day-to-day lives may further encourage participation and enthusiasm. For instance, if employees see that those who are skilled in ethical decision making are more likely to be promoted, they may be more motivated to participate in the training in order to gain similar skills.

Train-the-trainer

The same principles that apply to designing an effective training program also apply to designing an effective train-the-trainer program—the training designed for ethics trainers to learn and practice the material they will deliver to trainees. In essence, a successful training program requires the development of two trainings—one for the trainees and one for the trainers. Train-the-trainer sessions should include information on the background of the ethics training to provide trainers insight on why the training is important. Trainer buy-in may be important for keeping trainers engaged and communicating the importance of training to the trainees. As 'the face' of the ethics training, trainers' attitudes or beliefs are likely to be noticed by trainees and, thus, may impact how trainees view the training. Train-the-trainer sessions should also involve opportunities for trainers to practice delivering the content. As in other training efforts, trainers should receive feedback on their delivery. Providing trainers with a general script may be useful for guiding and standardizing training delivery across sessions and groups. Additionally, role modeling may be used to improve trainer performance, such that trainers can participate in other trainings, or watch a sample training by experienced trainers, to gain exposure to effective delivery techniques. It may also be useful for organizations to create a network of peer coaches internal to the organization who help coach employees on how to make an ethical decision and take ethical action (Gentile, 2008). In this instance, train-the-trainer sessions should also include coaching-related training, preparing the peer network for both the ethical issues they may be approached with, as well as interpersonal coaching-focused issues.

Scheduling

There are several logistical considerations when scheduling trainings. For example, when selecting a facility in which to hold the training, it is important to bear in mind the class size, or the number of trainees in each training session. Research suggests that larger class sizes that have more than 30 trainees may be as effective as smaller class sizes (e.g., Watts et al., 2017; Medeiros et al., 2017). However, when designing highly interactive training sessions with discussion and activities, larger class sizes may be difficult for a single trainer to manage. For example, if exercises include asking groups to share their collective responses, it will likely be difficult to hear from all of the groups in a large class. As such, we recommend capping the training size to around 40 trainees per session. However, the appropriate number of trainees may also depend on the duration of training. For instance, a 90-minute, intensive, highly interactive section with 40 trainees may not allow for the in-depth processing and discussions that are important for encouraging a lasting training impact. Instead, a session of that nature may require a small group to effectively execute those exercises in that timeframe. A careful consideration of the number of trainees is essential to allow for a diversity of views to be expressed while also maintaining a manageable number of trainees for the trainer. In this instance, a diversity of views may be important for trainees to understand the myriad views on ethics and related decisions that exist.

Once the number of trainees for each session has been decided, it is time to find a room suitable for that number, as well as one that is conducive to the selected delivery methods. At this point, it is important to consider the room configuration and other needs that may be important to effectively execute the training design. Additionally, the number of trainers should be considered at this point. For larger, more interactive sessions, we recommend having multiple trainers to effectively manage and facilitate the group (Watts et al., 2017). Lastly, do not forget to book the room!

Communicate positive results

Previous chapters have noted the importance of upper management support for ethics training efforts. As training continues, managers can continue to build this support by sharing the positive results of ethics training with relevant stakeholders. This is especially important if some stake-holders were hesitant to support the effort in the first place. Additionally, if positive results are observed in the pilot training sessions, these results can be shared with recent and future trainees to help demonstrate the effectiveness of the program and build further support among the trainee population. Building support helps foster motivation, which, in turn, encourages learning and application.

Investigate negative results

As noted previously, training improvements do not stop when the pilot training stops. It is critical to monitor the training program and its results to identify new issues as well as areas for improvement. Although the next chapter will discuss this in further detail, it is important to highlight here as well that training design is a continuous process. Results should be continuously reviewed throughout the duration of the program to catch any problems before they grow into larger concerns. This is especially true as time progresses, as organizational characteristics may change and new issues may emerge, resulting in the need for modifications to training content. Additionally, some research suggests that trainings such as sexual harassment and unconscious bias training may result in a backlash effect, meaning that the training results in the opposite of the desired effect. For instance, some sexual harassment training programs have shown to increase victim-blaming and the likelihood of sexual harassment (Dobbin & Kalev, 2019). Similarly, in a review of unconscious bias training, the Equality and Human Rights Commission (2018) found that unconscious bias training may strengthen biases if biases are presented as unchangeable.

Organizations must then carefully monitor results of their ethics training programs and carefully investigate what components or aspects of the program may be causing this effect. To investigate, ethics training managers could conduct surveys, interviews, or focus groups related to specific content at the end of each training session. Alternatively, ethics training managers could experimentally test the effects of different training components on the outcomes of interest. For example, ethics training managers might deliver only one module or section of the training to a few groups of trainees, asking them to complete the relevant evaluation after the module. If done for all modules, training managers may be able to detect where the training is going wrong. Regardless of how training managers go about reviewing training effectiveness, they should review results regularly. Depending on the frequency of training, reviews could take place at the end of each session, weekly, monthly, semiannually, or annually. Doing so allows for the detection of potential issues before they become serious problems. For instance, if signs of a backlash effect are observed after the first month of training sessions, continuing to implement the training in its current form may result in more harm than good. If undesirable results are observed, ethics training managers should consider temporarily pausing training efforts, identifying the problem, and revising the training as appropriate. Once issues have been addressed, it may be useful to then begin the pilot testing process again prior to launching the implementation process.

Planning for the unexpected

Although pilot testing helps to reduce the number of issues and errors that occur during training, problems will inevitably arise. It is important for ethics training managers to anticipate these potential problems and develop backup plans. For example, if training evaluation measures (e.g., surveys) are completed outside of the training environment and are optional, trainees are less likely to complete them. This may result in fewer responses by which to evaluate the training. In this instance, ethics training managers may seek out additional qualitative feedback such as descriptions of what went well or poorly and how trainees have applied what they have learned on the job. Specific trainees could also be approached to request that they complete the evaluation. However, if sensitive material is being collected, confidentiality should be ensured. Giving thought to issues such as this prior to their occurrence may allow for swifter responses and minimal interference. Thus, managers should give thought to potential issues that may arise in their specific training environment and organization, as well as planned responses in the event that they do.

To summarize, the list below provides a series of critical questions for managers to consider when planning ethics training efforts. We recommend creating a specific training plan that addresses each of these questions and details the more practical requirements for successful training implementation.

- What is my ethics training communication strategy?
- How will I train the trainers?
- How many trainees should be included in each session?
- What are the room, technology, trainer, and other requirements for each session?
- How will I share the results with the organization, including the trainees?
- What approach will I take if negative results are found?
- What backup and contingency plans are in place if plans do not unfold as expected?

Conclusion

It can be easy to miss flaws or potential issues in our own designs. Just as Richard Hendricks in Silicon Valley experienced, one's personal view of a training may cause them to miss the way users, or in this case trainees, view the program. Pilot testing provides a mechanism to safely and proactively test an ethics training program with different stakeholders, including both experts and trainees. By following the first two phases of pilot testing and carefully planning for implementation in phase 3, training designers can increase the likelihood that ethics training will be positively received and have the intended impact.

References

Dobbin, F., & Kalev, A. (2019). The promise and peril of sexual harassment programs. *Proceedings of the National Academy of Sciences of the United States of America*, 116(25), 12255–12260.

Equality and Human Rights Commission (2018). Unconscious bias training: An assessment of the evidence for effectiveness. Retrieved on January 31, 2019 from https://www.equalityhumanrights.com/sites/default/files/research-report-113-unconcious-bais-training-an-assessment-of-the-evidence-for-effectiveness-pdf.pdf.

Freiler, L. (May 31, 2019). Test strategy: Alpha vs. beta testing. Retrieved on January 31, 2019 from https://www.centercode.com/blog/2011/01/alpha-vs-beta-testing.

Gentile, M. (2013). Giving voice to values in the workplace: A practical approach to building moral competence. In L. E. Sekerka, (Ed.), *Ethics Training in Action: An Examination of Issues, Techniques, and Development*. Charlotte, NC: Information Age Publishing.

Krueger, J. (1998). Enhancement bias in descriptions of self and others. *Personality and Social Psychology Bulletin, 24*, 505–516.

Medeiros, K. E., Watts, L. L., Mulhearn, T. J., Steele, L. M., Mumford, M. D., & Connelly, S. (2017). What is working, what is not, and what we need to know: A meta-analytic review of business ethics instruction. *Journal of Academic Ethics, 15*, 245–275.

Noe, R. A. (1986). Trainees' attributes and attitudes: Neglected influences on training effectiveness. *Academy of Management Review, 11*, 736–749.

Onarheim, B., & Christensen, B. T. (2012). Distributed idea screening in stage-gate development processes. *Journal of Engineering Design, 23*, 660–673.

Quinones, M. A. (1995). Pretraining context effects: Training assignment as feedback. *Journal of Applied Psychology, 80*, 226–238.

Tavel, J. A., & Fosdick, L. (2001). Closeout of four phase II vanguard trials and patient rollover into a large international phase III HIV clinical endpoint trial. *Controlled Clinical Trials, 22*, 42–48.

Thabane, L., Ma, J., Chu, R., Cheng, J., Ismaila, A., Rios, L. P., Robson, R., Thabane, M., Giangregorio, L., & Goldsmith, C. H. (2010). A tutorial on pilot studies: The what, why and how. *BMC Medical Research Methodology, 10*, 1–10.

Tobias, S. (June 19, 2016). 'Silicon Valley' season 3, episode 9: What exactly is Pied Piper? Retrieved on January 31, 2019 from https://www.nytimes.com/2016/06/19/arts/television/silicon-valley-season-3-episode-9-recap.html.

Van Teijlingen, E. R., & Hundley, V. (2001). The importance of pilot studies. *Social Research Update, 35*, 1–4.

Watts, L. L., Medeiros, K. E., Mulhearn, T. J., Steele, L. M., Connelly, S., & Mumford, M. D. (2017). Are ethics training programs improving? A meta-analytic review of past and present ethics instruction in the sciences. *Ethics & Behavior, 27*, 351–384.

11

PROGRAM MONITORING AND REFINEMENT

Tristan J. McIntosh

***

You go to the doctor for your annual physical each year, or at least you know you *should*. Doing so allows your doctor to make sure your body is functioning properly, diagnose and provide treatment if something is wrong, and make adjustments to your overall health care management plan. Similarly, routinely giving an ethics training program a 'check up' will ensure that it is operating as it should and that it covers relevant content. With the appropriate diagnostic tools and approach, ethics training managers will be able to detect program deficiencies and make corrective modifications as needed. In what follows, we highlight helpful practices for monitoring and refining an ethics training program.

Adopting the right mindset

Once an ethics training program has been carefully developed and implemented, it is not sufficient to let the program exist in perpetuity without any modification. Ethics training is not a one-and-done ordeal. This is not to say that ethics training programs need to be undergoing constant change. Rather, ethics training should be undergoing constant monitoring with the opportunity for periodic changes to various program elements. To monitor an ethics training program effectively, managers can benefit from adopting a continuous learning and improvement mindset. This mindset is characterized by constantly striving to improve and change (Locke & Jain, 1995). By acknowledging that an ethics training program will never achieve permanent perfection, ethics training managers can take steps to be proactive in monitoring the environment in which the training is embedded and the effectiveness of the ethics training program itself.

What makes an ethics training program successful at one point in time may not be as effective later. Societal norms and laws change. Institutional norms and policies change. Employees working at an organization change. New knowledge and information become available over time. As a result of these changes, the content and logistics of ethics training programs should be updated to reflect these shifts. To make impactful changes to ethics training, a variety of sources of data can be used as an indicator for what should be changed and how it should be changed. These data sources are discussed in detail throughout this chapter.

In addition to providing evidence for program effectiveness, routinely collecting evaluation data can also provide information about when the ethics training program may require modification and refinement. If the effectiveness of an ethics training program declines, organizations should investigate the source of the ineffectiveness and adjust training content and delivery accordingly. Below, we discuss strategies for monitoring factors internal and external to an organization that may influence training effectiveness and that may provide helpful clues as to what training program elements should be adjusted.

Internal monitoring

Several elements within an organization may influence ethics training effectiveness and impact. These elements internal to an organization can signal when changes to an ethics training program are needed. Many data-driven internal monitoring strategies exist that can indicate when changes of this nature are warranted. Understanding what these elements are can help training program managers be preventive in their approach to ethics training program development, implementation, and impact. These elements are described in detail below.

Routine assessments of training impact

As mentioned in Chapter 6, obtaining evaluation data at the conclusion of training can provide an indication of training effectiveness and training elements that might require modification. Evaluation data can also be collected during training. Doing so provides information on specific program components (e.g., active learning activities) in real time as trainees are exposed to them. Trainee reaction data can provide insights as to what elements of the training program are perceived less favorably by employees. Program elements that are not viewed positively may hinder the magnitude of impact that a training program has within an organization (Turner et al., 2018). Therefore, negative reactions to certain training elements signal the need to change some element of training program content or delivery. In another example, assessing trainee ethical knowledge or skill acquisition can provide insight as to what trainees learned during training, as well as the areas where gaps remain.

Beyond collecting evaluation data immediately following a training program, assessing trainee knowledge and skills periodically long after training has taken place can help ethics training managers understand what trainees retain from ethics training in the long term. Moreover, longitudinal assessment, or assessing trainees periodically over a period of time, can provide information about the lasting impact of ethics training on trainees. Put differently, periodically assessing trainees several weeks, months, and even years following formal ethics training can signal to managers when a refresher ethics training is needed. For example, a refresher training may be needed if employees scored high on a measure that assesses knowledge of regulatory requirements immediately following training but scored considerably lower after taking a follow-up assessment 1 year after training. Refresher trainings are discussed further at the end of this chapter.

Organizational surveying

The post-training work environment influences the long-term effectiveness of an ethics training program (see Chapter 9). Training transfer, which occurs when trainees regularly apply what they learned during training to their jobs (Broad & Newstrom, 1992), is a critical element for long-term effectiveness of an ethics training program. Specifically, the transfer of knowledge and skills learned during ethics training can be affected by numerous factors, including whether employees have opportunities to practice what was learned during ethics training, if leadership supports what was taught during ethics training, and if employees perceive whether an ethical institutional climate exists (Aguinis & Kraiger, 2009; Kraiger, Ford, & Salas, 1993). Assessing such factors in the post-training work environment can provide information about the likelihood of ethics training having its intended impact. It can also provide information to ethics training managers about changes that may need to be made to both ethics training content and in the post-training work environment. For example, if data from an organization-wide ethics culture survey indicate that employees in certain departments perceive the culture in their department as unethical, this may signal that targeted ethics training is needed for leaders within those departments (see Chapter 5).

Organizations that document the frequency and nature of reports made about unethical behavior by employees can monitor if the number of instances of unethical behavior increases or decreases over time, whether certain unethical behaviors tend to be repeated even after corrective action is taken, and how severe reports of wrongdoing are. In addition to preventing ethical scandals from unfolding within an organization, this information can signal when additional ethics training is needed for employees or when revisions to an ethics training program are needed. For example, if reports of unethical work practices increase in frequency over time, this may indicate that an ethics training program is not having the intended effect, and that revisions to training content or changes in the work environment are needed (Mumford, Steele, & Watts, 2015). However, it is important to note that it is common, once ethics training programs are in place, for employees to be more likely to report unethical behavior. This is due to increases in ethical sensitivity as a function of having taken the ethics training (Clarkeburn, 2002). That is, unethical behavior becomes more salient and noticeable to employees. Therefore, ethics training program managers should not panic if reports of unethical behavior increase after an ethics training program is in place. Rather, this increase can be a signal that the ethics training program is improving the ethical awareness of employees. Over time, the number of formally re-ported unethical incidents should decrease as employees become more cognizant of how to speak up and take ethical action on a day-to-day basis.

Changes in employees

It is expected that the makeup of an organization's workforce will change over time. Employees retire, quit, or change roles within an organization. When employees leave an organization, this is an excellent opportunity to conduct exit interviews, asking about ethical issues, lapses, or gaps they noticed during their time at the organization. Doing so can identify areas where ethics training content could be focused. To replace employees leaving the organization, organizations must hire new employees, often many at once. As part of the onboarding process, new employees are often required to take trainings to learn about the organization's norms and policies. Having new employees take part in an organization's ethics training program should be no exception. It is likely that new employees will have knowledge and skill gaps related to ethics within a particular organizational setting, and providing them with the same ethics training that all other employees received will ensure that expectations about ethical behavior are communicated to everyone and that employees are provided with the same information about the organization's ethical policies and norms. This will ensure that the effects of an organization's ethics training program are reaching all incoming employees.

An astute ethics training manager will monitor the volume and makeup (e.g., skills, areas of expertise, age) of incoming employees to see if the focus of certain ethics training content needs to shift to meet the needs of new employees. For example, an organization that has recently hired a large amount of young employees, or employees where this is their first job, may find that these individuals lack industry experience and knowl-edge of ethical norms and, therefore, may need ethics training to sup-plement this lack of knowledge and provide a foundation for behaving ethically in a professional environment. In contrast, when hiring more experienced employees who have decades of industry experience, providing ethics training that emphasizes 'this is the way things are done around here' when it comes to ethics-related issues can ensure bad habits do not carry over from prior roles at other organizations. This also provides an opportunity to explicitly state expectations for ethical behavior. These differences between novice and seasoned employees may warrant additions or modifications to ethics training program content.

Changes in organizational policies and procedures

To reflect shifts in technology, improve processes and efficiency, and respond to societal changes, organizations may add or modify policies and procedures. These policy and procedure changes require that employees modify their behaviors and practices, and these changes may have implications for the ethical conduct of employees. For example, an organization may institute a new policy that mandates employees to not spend over a certain amount of money pursuing clients. Especially if there were no prior rules about how much could be spent on client pursuits, some employees may experience challenges with navigating client pursuits. In particular, some employees may feel pressured to meet client quotas and may experience internal conflict due to competing goals (i.e., complying with new policy versus meeting client quotas).

To ensure that employees are capable of navigating these changes and dilemmas and to ensure that employees understand the implications of new policies and procedures, especially those with ethical implications, ethics training content may need to be added or revised when new policies and procedures are put into place. Changes can include adding new training modules, activities, facilitated discussions, or talking points related to new policies and their implications. Doing so will make sure employees are aware of what the change means for them and provide employees with the skills needed to navigate the ethical and professional issues involved with adhering to new policies and procedures.

Changes in organizational goals

The vision and mission of an organization often direct the short- and long-term goals sought by individuals within the organization. It is not uncommon for these goals to shift over time, especially if an organization enters a new industry or expands into niche areas of the current industry in which they specialize. The prioritization and introduction of new goals may present unique risks for unethical behavior to occur, especially because there may be ethical considerations unique to new industries that current organizational employees might be unaware of. For example, if an organization sets a goal to innovate in a field or market where it has not traditionally innovated, it may try to achieve and implement these innovations quickly before fully understanding the ethical norms and standards of that field or market, and, subsequently, the consequences of the innovation. It may also be the case that, as a function of new goals being championed by leaders in an organization, employees feel pressure to behave in certain ways to attain those goals. These risks can be mitigated, in part, by providing up-to-date ethics training for employees.

Table 11.1 provides a list of practical questions that ethics training program managers can use as a guide when engaging in internal monitoring techniques.

External monitoring

In addition to monitoring internal organizational factors, it is equally critical to monitor the broader external environment with an organization's ethics training program in mind. Below we discuss sources of external information that can signal when ethics training content or other training program elements should be refined, removed, or added.

New norms

Organizations operate as an integral part of society, which means that adherence to certain standards and norms is expected. As inevitable cultural and societal shifts take place over time, organizations often institute certain policies or procedures in response to these shifts. For example, there has been a recent movement where consumers want to buy from and do business with organizations that are perceived as socially responsible (Neilsen Global Corporate Sustainability Report, 2015). Corporate social responsibility is marked by an organization taking a public stance on addressing social or environmental issues (Porter & Kramer, 2006). In

Table 11.1 Practical Questions to Consider for Internal Monitoring

Key Considerations	Questions
Routine assessments of training impact	• What evaluation measures make sense to administer periodically after ethics training? • How often will evaluation measures be administered after ethics training has ended?
Organizational surveying	• What types of information do you want to gather for an organizational survey? • Who and how many people will take part in the organizational survey? • At what point will the organizational survey take place?
Changes in employees	• What is your organization's turnover rate? • How many new hires have been made recently? • What proportion of employees have much or little work experience?
Changes in organizational policies and procedures	• What organizational policies and procedures have recently been put into place? • Are there any policies and procedures that employees may perceive as conflicting with one another?
Changes in organizational goals	• Has upper management communicated any forthcoming changes or additions to your organization's goals? • What competencies do employees need to ethically carry out your organization's goals?

response to this market pressure toward corporate social responsibility, organizations may adopt new policies and practices. For example, organizations may implement environmentally friendly business operations, dedicate a portion of their profits to provide resources to underserved groups, or implement policies that support employee well-being.

In relation to updating an ethics training program, shifts in societal norms may point to the need for a change in the learning objectives of a training program, the content of cases used in training activities, or the content of guided discussions that take place during training. For example, with the advent of big data and concerns about privacy, tech companies may choose to focus a portion of the content in their ethics training programs on ethical uses of technology or ethical considerations about data mining or artificial intelligence.

New legislation and regulations

Similar to changes in societal norms, changes to federal and state legislation or updates to field-specific regulations and guidelines may obligate organizations to update their policies and procedures. Ethics training content may need to be updated to bring employees up to speed on these policy and procedural changes. Many legal changes may have implications for both ethics and compliance in organizations. For example, in 2002, the Sarbanes–Oxley Act was passed after multiple corporate financial scandals became public in the early 2000s (e.g., Enron; Sarbanes–Oxley Act, 2002). The Sarbanes–Oxley Act mandates that corporate executives take full responsibility and accountability for the accuracy of financial reports. As part of upholding this law, organizations may choose to add a unit to their ethics training program that highlights the importance of accuracy in reporting financial information and educates employees how to be compliant and ethical in this regard. In another example, the California Consumer Privacy Act (CCPA) recently went into effect on January 1, 2020, and was created to provide individual consumers with more control over their personal data and information. This law requires organizations to modify their data collection practices, including disclosing the amount and type of personal information collected, providing individuals with the option to opt out of sharing their data, and making individuals aware when there has been a data breach (Piovesan, 2019). Organizations may include a training module focused on ethical issues with data privacy in response to this new legislation.

Adapting to changes in the market

Organizations do not operate in isolation. Rather, they are part of a broader environment full of competitors, customers, and various other stakeholders. Changes made by these stakeholders can signal to organizations what and when they need to change in order to remain competitive and relevant. For example, consider 23andMe and Ancestry.com, which are both organizations that specialize in genealogy and DNA testing. As competitors, each organization must distinguish themselves from the other and release new, more exciting products. There is obvious pressure to innovate. This pressure could, in turn, unintentionally encourage unethical behavior or corner-cutting on the part of employees. However, consumers are more likely to purchase from organizations they identify as trustworthy and ethical (Accenture, 2018). Given the genetics and data-based nature of the products sold by these two organizations, ethical issues related to data management, data sharing, and privacy should be addressed. If one of these organizations were to champion ethics initiatives related to these particular ethical issues, and it was received favorably by consumers, the other organization may then seek to improve their own ethics initiatives to retain market share.

Ethical scandals in other organizations

In addition to monitoring what other organizations are doing well with their ethics training initiatives, it is also wise to monitor what other organizations are not doing well when it comes to ethics. Specifically, taking note of and learning lessons from ethical scandals that take place at other organizations can sound an alarm to other organizations and indicate that more preventive measures may need to be taken to avoid such a scandal. Moreover, details about ethical scandals can be used as case studies in ethics training, and organizations may wish to add this learning activity to bolster the impact that training has on trainees (McWilliams & Nahavandi, 2006). When implementing these case studies in ethics training, trainees identify the causes of the scandal, discuss what could have been done differently, and deliberate about what steps can be taken to prevent a similar issue from happening in the future. This case study approach is both relatable and relevant to trainees, as it aligns a real-world example with the learning objectives of the ethics training.

Table 11.2 provides a list of practical questions that can help guide ethics training managers with the use of external monitoring techniques.

Refresher training

As referenced throughout this chapter, shifts both within and outside of an organization may, over time, result in ethics training content that becomes outdated. With these shifts, the ethical knowledge and skills of employees are at risk of becoming obsolete, potentially contributing to sub-optimal ethical decision making. Employees may also forget what

Table 11.2 Practical Questions to Consider for External Monitoring

Key Considerations	Questions
New norms	• Have there been any recent shifts in societal norms that may affect what is viewed as ethical?
New legislation and regulations	• Have any rules or regulations changed in a way that impacts the decision making of employees? • Have any rules or regulations changed in a way that impacts what is viewed as ethical?
Adapting to changes in the market	• Have peer companies or competitors made any substantial changes to the ethics policies and practices at their organization? • Have peer companies or competitors been publicly recognized for ethics? What have they done to deserve this recognition?
Ethical scandals in other organizations	• Have there been any recent ethical scandals at similar organizations? • What lessons should be incorporated into ethics training concerning past scandals in other organizations?

was learned during ethics training over time. Refresher trainings are key to the retention of this knowledge and skills (Salas, Tannenbaum, Kraiger, & Smith-Jentsch, 2012). Therefore, it is not uncommon for organizations to mandate that employees take a refresher ethics training when a certain amount of time has lapsed since the employee took the ethics training last or when major updates to ethics training content have been made since the employee took the ethics training. In order for an ethics training initiative to be wholly effective, the majority of, if not all, employees need to possess the same foundational ethical knowledge, skills, and attitudes. Re-training employees helps make employees the best ethical performers possible and helps avoid complacency. Routine, ethics-focused conversations between employees that occur beyond formal training further reinforce ethical thinking and action by employees.

Refresher ethics trainings have the added benefit of signaling to employees that upper management at an organization values ethics. That is, refresher ethics trainings communicate that ethics training is not an activity done just to 'check the box.' Rather, refresher training allows organizations to keep up with the latest trends and research in the domain of organizational ethics without having to 'start from scratch.' Refresher ethics trainings can be shorter and less of a time and resource burden than initial ethics training efforts. Refresher trainings can even be framed as an element of continuing professional development, which is likely to be of value to employees seeking to grow professionally and enhance their ethical skillset. Further, refresher ethics trainings can motivate employees to take appropriate action in response to ethically charged situations and remind employees of the organization's core values.

The frequency in administration of refresher ethics trainings may vary depending on the dynamism and complexity of a job. Those with jobs in highly dynamic fields where norms, policies, and regulations change rapidly need to take refresher trainings on specialty topics more frequently (e.g., quarterly) to stay up-to-date, as opposed to those with more routine jobs that seldom change. Similarly, employees who are required to retain a great deal of ethics and compliance-related information may need to take refresher trainings more regularly to reduce the amount of content crammed into a single training and help remind employees about specific details that might be easily forgotten (McDaniel, Fadler, & Pashler, 2013). Additionally, refresher trainings may be needed more frequently if new or unique ethics issues emerge or if employees seldom use critical information or skills taught during ethics training. In this case, refresher ethics trainings can help employees keep their minds sharp and alert when it comes to navigating ethical issues that only rarely occur within a field or organization.

As changes are made to ethics training content and as different employees participate in different versions of ethics training within an organization, it is important to maintain detailed documentation about these changes. This organized record keeping can help ethics training program managers keep track of what was changed and when. This information may be useful later on when making decisions about who should take refresher training and what content that refresher training should cover.

Conclusion

In this chapter, we identified internal and external factors that managers should attend to when monitoring and refining ethics training programs. Specifically, internal organizational changes, such as policy changes or shifts in an organization's goals, and external changes, such as new legislation or shifts in societal norms, can signal when and what changes to ethics training content should be made to maximize effectiveness. When substantial changes to the content of an ethics training have been made, or when a substantial amount of time has passed since employees have taken training, a refresher ethics training is warranted.

This chapter also highlights the need for a continuous improvement mindset, which is essential for ethics training program managers in order to adapt to the constant changes in the internal and external environments. By routinely monitoring environmental changes that could lessen the effectiveness of existing training, and modifying ethics training accordingly, ethics training initiatives will be set up for long-term success.

References

Accenture. (2018). From me to we: The rise of the purpose-led brand. Retrieved from https://www.accenture.com/gb-en/insights/strategy/brand-pu rpose?c=strat_competitiveagilnovalue_10437228&n=mrl_1118.

Aguinis, H., & Kraiger, K. (2009). Benefits of training and development for individuals and teams, organizations, and society. *Annual Review of Psychology, 60,* 451–474.

Broad, M. L., & Newstrom, J. W. (1992). *Transfer of training.* Reading, MA: Addison-Wesley.

Clarkeburn, H. (2002). A test for ethical sensitivity in science. *Journal of Moral Education, 31,* 439–453.

Kraiger, K., Ford, J. K., & Salas, E. (1993). Application of cognitive, skill-based, and affective theories of learning outcomes to new methods of training evaluation. *Journal of Applied Psychology, 78,* 311–328.

Locke, E. A., & Jain, V. K. (1995). Organizational learning and continuous improvement. *The International Journal of Organizational Analysis, 3,* 45–68.

McDaniel, M. A., Fadler, C. L., & Pashler, H. (2013). Effects of spaced versus massed training in function learning. *Journal of Experimental Psychology: Learning, Memory, and Cognition, 39,* 1417–1432.

McWilliams, V., & Nahavandi, A. (2006). Using live cases to teach ethics. *Journal of Business Ethics, 67,* 421–433.

Mumford, M. D., Steele, L., & Watts, L. L. (2015). Evaluating ethics education programs: A multilevel approach. *Ethics & Behavior, 25,* 37–60.

Neilsen Global Sustainability Report (2015). *The sustainability imperative.* Retrieved on January 31, 2019, from https://www.nielsen.com/us/en/insights/report/2015/the-sustainability-imperative-2/.

Piovesan, C. (2019). How privacy laws are changing to protect personal information. *Forbes.* Retrieved on January 31, 2019 from https://www.forbes.com/sites/cognitiveworld/2019/04/05/how-privacy-laws-are-changing-to-protect-personal-information/#2674594b753d.

Porter, M. E., & Kramer, M. R. (2006). The link between competitive advantage and corporate social responsibility. *Harvard Business Review, 84,* 78–92.

Sarbanes Oxley Act. (2002). Conference report (to accompany H.R. 3763). Pub. L. No. 107-204, 116. Stat 745. Washington, D.C.: U.S. G.P.O.

Salas, E., Tannenbaum, S. I., Kraiger, K., & Smith-Jentsch, K. A. (2012). The science of training and development in organizations: What matters in practice. *Psychological Science in the Public Interest, 13,* 74–101.

Turner, M. R., Watts, L. L., Steele, L. M., Mulhearn, T. J., Torrence, B. S., Todd, E. M., & Connelly, S. (2018). How did you like this course? The advantages and limitations of reaction criteria in ethics education. *Ethics & Behavior, 28,* 483–496.

12

GOING GLOBAL WITH ETHICS TRAINING

Kelsey E. Medeiros

***

There are some skills you need to handle the Americans. How can we take advantage of American characteristics to make them work for Fuyao. There's a culture in the US where children are showered with encouragement. So everyone who grows up in the US is overconfident. They are super confident. Americans love being flattered to death. We need to use our wisdom to guide them and help them. Because we are better than them.

–Chinese leader, *American Factory*

The Chinese really don't help us out at all. They just walk around and tell the Americans what to do. Do this and you're like, why. They don't tell you why at all. They walk away.

–American worker, *American Factory*

The impact of globalization on business practices requires little introduction given its ubiquity in modern society. The media regularly highlights the challenges of a globalized society and the inherent clashes associated with cross-cultural ventures. Recently, the documentary, *American Factory* (Richert, Benello, and Bognar, 2019), brought special attention to these issues with a close look at Fuyao—a Chinese manufacturing company employing both Chinese and American workers in China and the United States of America (USA). As the introductory chapter quotes suggest, the Chinese and American workers held contrasting beliefs about work, values, and one another. Although the documentary focused specifically on the relationship between cultural differences and employee performance, safety, and union-related outcomes, differing cultural beliefs and perspectives can also lead to ethical challenges—challenges that significantly impact how ethics training should be designed and delivered.

The importance of understanding the cultural environment for which you are designing a training is underscored by research exploring how cultural differences impact ethical outcomes. Research on cross-cultural ethics consistently demonstrates key differences in attitudes, awareness, and action across cultures. For example, a team of researchers was interested in the relationship between culture and attitudes toward business ethics and questionable business practices such as bribery, padding expense accounts, and discrimination. To study this, they conducted a survey of 345 managers enrolled in Executive MBA programs in the USA, India, and Korea. They found significantly different attitudes toward business ethics in general, as well as on nine of the twelve specific practices they investigated (Christie, Kwon, Stoeberl, & Baumhart, 2003). For example, India and Korea viewed the marketing of unhealthy products differently, while India and the USA viewed harming the environment and complying with a superior's orders differently. The authors were able to link these differences to underlying traits distinctive of each country's culture. When developing an ethics training intended to span multiple countries and cultures, ethics training managers are then faced with the challenge of which views to emphasize and how to manage discrepancies.

Along these lines, researchers have also investigated reactions to potential ethics interventions, finding cultural differences in employee perceptions of a proposed ethics intervention's effectiveness (Becker &

Fritzsche, 1987). Cultural differences also appear related to the way we perceive, process, and take action in response to an ethical issue. For example, a team of researchers conducted a survey to examine cultural differences in levels of concern for morality and ethical judgments in the USA, Eastern Europe, and Indonesia. They found that the cultural context impacted how individuals responded to a hypothetical ethical case (Davis, Johnson, & Ohmer, 1998). The researchers emphasized that, in this instance, cultural differences were likely due to differing ethical priorities across cultures at that time. For example, respondents from the USA were particularly sensitive to sexual harassment issues in comparison to respondents from other regions. This was likely due to sexual-harassment related events occurring at that time within the USA, highlighting the susceptibility of ethical perceptions and decisions to culturally significant events (Davis et al., 1998).

For ethics training managers who work internationally, cultural differences such as these can pose a major challenge. So far in this book, we have highlighted several ethics training practices that have shown to be effective, but much of this discussion remains embedded in a Western perspective. The same principles and practices of ethics training design may prove less effective in other areas of the world. For example, the previous chapters have advocated for a formal approach to ethics training and related practices. However, as Gary Weaver at the University of Delaware suggested, these same techniques may face backlash in a country such as the Philippines where workers tend to be skeptical of formal practices and interventions (Weaver, 2001). Instead, a more informal approach, such as mentoring programs or unstructured discussion groups, may have a stronger impact. The potential for variations in training effectiveness due to cultural differences extends beyond this example of the Philippines and impacts the way ethics training is designed in each country. Ethics training managers must then understand how underlying cultural characteristics impact the effectiveness of ethics interventions globally.

As we explore these differences in this chapter, we emphasize that our goal is not to identify a right or wrong way of responding to specific issues. Rather, we hope to highlight cultural sensitivities and the related practical implications for ethics training. We hope this helps ethics training managers make informed decisions regarding how ethics trainings can be developed and delivered within a cultural context to maximize effectiveness. We distinguish the views presented in this chapter from a relativist perspective which argues that there are no universal moral principles but, instead, that enacting moral principles may require different approaches and skills given different cultural contexts (Forsyth, 1980). The aim of this chapter is not to champion a particular philosophical perspective. Instead, this chapter aims to highlight that employees and organizations operate within a cultural reality that should be considered and leveraged when designing a training or ethics intervention to facilitate a long-term impact.

Research on cross-cultural differences uses generalizations, or stereotypes, about how people tend to think, feel, and act across countries. This does not mean that everyone within the same country, or culture, is expected to hold the same views. However, just as there is often a grain of truth to many stereotypes, the generalizations discussed in this chapter have been found to show up reliably when studying different cultures across many decades of research (Hofstede, 2002). Drawing on this research, we suggest a general framework to understand how different cultures across the globe may perceive and respond to ethics training differently. Although a full exploration of specific cultures and their ethical philosophies and legal practices falls outside the scope of this chapter, broad inferences regarding cultural differences in ethical approaches are drawn to provide meaningful implications for designing effective ethics programs.

Legal differences

One does not have to look far to see legal differences across countries. Countries differ in their legal definitions and expectations regarding safety, human rights, and privacy with each legal perspective influencing what citizens of that country view as appropriate or inappropriate. As noted in Chapter 2, a key component of ethical decision making is adhering to relevant laws and standards. Working internationally blurs this requirement, leaving employees left to wonder—which legal requirements should I follow?

At the time of writing this chapter, perhaps one of the most prominent examples of legal differences is the issue of data privacy. At present, in an effort to protect the public's data, the European Union (EU) operates under the General Data Protection Regulation (GDPR) which dictates how customer or consumer data can be used (International Commissioner's Office, 2020). This explains why websites accessed within an EU country prompt users to review a summary of how that website is using their data and to either agree or disagree to the terms of use. Some regions in the USA have adopted similar policies (e.g., California), however, no such policy currently exists at the federal level. As another example, both the UK and the USA have adopted anti-bribery policies, with the USA enacting the Foreign Corrupt Practices Act (FCPA) in 1977 and the UK enacting the UK Bribery Act in 2010. Although similar in concept, the UK Bribery is one of the strictest anti-bribery legislations in the world (Transparency International UK, n.d.). In both instances, when organizations operate in countries with stricter legislation, they must adhere to the relevant rules and regulations—even when they go beyond the standard operating procedures or regulations of their home country. Thus, when a US company is conducting business in the UK, US employees must adhere to the UK's Bribery Act regulations. Similarly, when conducting business in the EU, US employees must adhere to regulations outlined by the GDPR.

The challenge, however, arises when a conflict exists between a home and host country's regulations, with the host country's policies being more lenient than the home country's regulations. Take, for example, the dilemma regarding working conditions and pay for workers in countries such as Bangladesh, where the minimum wage is low compared to global standards (Butler, 2019). Many companies operate in countries like Bangladesh because of the financial benefit stemming from cheap labor and fewer safety regulations. Although such business practices may be legal in the host country, one has to question if these practices are ethical (e.g., Ethical Trading Initiative).

Although legal differences do exist, there are also fundamental principles of human rights established by the United Nations that have generally been accepted by many countries across the globe. These principles argue that states and organizations must 'protect, respect, and remedy' human rights. Specifically, states are expected to protect human rights through legal requirements and have the charge to remedy any issues that may arise, while businesses are expected to respect human rights by abiding by these requirements (United Nations, 2011). The agreed-upon human rights were established in the Universal Declaration of Human Rights

(1948) and include rights such as freedom from slavery, torture, and forced marriage. Additionally, it includes the right to work, equal pay, and an adequate standard of living. Although not all countries have adopted this framework, these rights are generally agreed upon and drive many decisions internationally.

The impact of these legal similarities and differences for ethics training in companies operating internationality is then clear—ethics training must include content focused on both legal similarities, differences, and the organization's policies and expectations on how to handle discrepancies in regulations. One way to do this is to establish and emphasize an organization's Code of Conduct, which outlines how employees should respond to particular ethical dilemmas (Stajkovic & Luthans, 1997). It may also involve highlighting pathways for seeking guidance in resolving these issues. Beyond the legal and content perspective, however, there are also cultural differences that may impact ethics training decisions when designing an internationally relevant ethics training program.

Cultural differences

A survey of 202 CEOs and Human Resource Professionals conducted by Right Management revealed that only 58% of managerial overseas assignments were judged as successful (Right Management, 2013). Much of this is likely due to the lack of preparation provided to managers moving oversees. For instance, the same survey found that only 25% of organizations offered training on cultural differences and that approximately 16% of organizations provided either no training or minimal training for managers moving abroad. Given the complexities of cultural differences, these numbers are troubling. A lack of awareness and preparation for how to manage cross-cultural differences when working internationally can lead to serious issues for managers—including ethics issues.

For companies operating in more than one country, designing a single ethics training that can be applied internationally will likely prove ineffective. In addition to the legal differences discussed previously, countries differ in their cultural values, norms, and perspectives, which can influence how business is conducted. More central to this book, however, these cultural differences can influence how training is designed and received by trainees around the globe.

The following discussion is intended to shed light on cultural differences that may impact training effectiveness when designing ethics trainings internationally. It bears noting that this discussion is not intended to say that organizations should attempt to radically change the cultural viewpoints of the countries in which they are training, but instead, that the training exists in a larger cultural ecosystem which can impact how trainees respond to the content and exercises presented. Take, for example, an organization that is interested in encouraging employees in a highly competitive culture, such as the USA where people are typically assertive and want to climb their way to the top, to make ethical decisions slowly and to put the needs of others before themselves. Doing so in this cultural environment may prove more challenging and require a different framing than encouraging employees to do the same in a more collaborative and group-focused culture, such as Sweden, where taking time to consider the needs of others is common practice. In order to maximize impact, the training designed or selected by ethics training managers may need to differ by culture so that the training framework aligns with the broader organizational and societal systems in which it operates.

Cultural dimensions

To understand cultural differences in ethics, we must first understand how cultures differ more broadly. A framework for understanding culture first arose in the 1970s thanks to the work of a Dutch psychologist by the name of Geert Hofstede (Hofstede, 1980). As the founder of the personnel research department at IBM Europe in the late 1960s, Hofstede investigated cultural differences in national values across this multinational corporation. His surveys included responses from nearly 120,000 IBM employees across 50 countries. This initial work resulted in the identification of cultural dimensions that explained the underlying 'personality' of a country or culture. Over the years, Hofstede, along with other researchers, have continued this work, now claiming six fundamental dimensions of cultural personalities: individualism, uncertainty avoidance, power distance, task-person orientation, long-term orientation, and indulgence (Chinese Culture Connection, 1987; Hofstede, Hofstede, & Minkov, 2010). Like individual personalities, a country falls along a spectrum of each of these traits where it can be high, low, or somewhere in-between. This is used to create a descriptive cultural personality profile representing a country's cultural personality.

Individualism

Individualism refers to the extent to which individuals take an interest in the goals of their broader group compared to their personal goals alone. In more individualistic societies, such as the USA, Australia, and the UK, people typically feel primarily responsible for themself and their immediate family. People in more individualistic societies are often interested in their personal goals and gains rather than the goal of the larger societal group. In contrast, those in more collectivist societies, such as China, India, and Japan, view their responsibility to one another more broadly, considering their responsibility to others in communities outside of their immediate family. People in collectivist societies also place a larger emphasis on the goals of the group rather than the individual.

When considering potential implications for ethics, people in collectivistic cultures will consider a wider range of stakeholder perspectives, as well as the impact of their decisions on people outside of their immediate family, compared to those working in more individualistic cultures (Husted & Allen, 2008). From an ethics training point of view, how one designs training materials can enhance or counteract this way of thinking. For instance, if using a case-based approach, asking questions about the case such as 'How does this dilemma impact you personally?' or 'What are the implications of this decision for your team, department, organization, and society?' may further engrain an individualistic or collectivistic perspective. The first question may encourage those in a collectivistic society to consider personal implications while the second question may encourage those in an individualistic society to consider the needs of the group.

Uncertainty avoidance

Uncertainty avoidance refers to how members of a society feel about ambiguity (Hofstede, 2001). Individuals in societies such as Greece, Japan, and South Korea, which are highly adverse to uncertainty, tend to be uncomfortable with ambiguity and prefer to deal with known futures and outcomes. In contrast, cultures that feel comfortable moving forward without knowing the outcomes for certain or needing to control their future include India, the USA, and China. Those cultures that avoid uncertainty are more likely to adhere to a strict set of codes, whereas those more comfortable with uncertainty may be more flexible in their adoption and implementation of rules and policies.

With respect to ethics training, encouraging employees from cultures that prefer to avoid uncertainty to embrace the ambiguity associated with ethical dilemmas may be met with resistance. This may be problematic as ethical dilemmas are oftentimes complex (see Chapter 2). A lack of attention to the subtleties and complexities of an ethical dilemma may result in unethical decisions (Watts, Medeiros, McIntosh, & Mulhearn, 2020). Individuals in these cultures may respond more favorably to a more compliance-focused approach but may need increased attention on skills and tools that can be used to navigate the ambiguity of ethical decision making. In comparison, employees from cultures that are more comfortable with uncertainty may be more open to ethical ambiguity and have no problem accepting this way of thinking about dilemmas. These same individuals, however, may struggle with applying a strict set of rules that those in high uncertainty-avoidance cultures are drawn to. In contrast to the earlier example, these individuals may prefer a training that allows them to navigate the complexities of an ethical dilemma but may need extra support in understanding the importance and application of relevant rules and guidelines.

Power distance

Power distance refers to how individuals perceive and respond to the distribution of power and authority within their society (Hofstede, 2001). Those in high power-distance cultures, such as Malaysia, Hong Kong, and France, are more sensitive to social hierarchies and may be more likely to follow the directives of someone who is higher up in the chain of command. Conversely, those in lower power-distance societies, such as the UK, USA, and the Netherlands, may be more willing to challenge authority or move forward on a decisive issue without requesting permission or seeking input from more senior leaders.

A society's power distance will likely impact whether or not employees feel comfortable challenging unethical orders passed down the chain of command (Weaver, 2001). Specifically, those in high power-distance societies may be less likely to challenge or call out those in positions of power when behaving unethically or handing down instructions that may result in employees behaving unethically. When it comes to ethics training, suggesting to employees in high power-distance societies that they should go against the orders of their supervisor will likely be met with strong resistance. The same suggestion, however, may face fewer challenges in a low power-distance society where challenging those in power is less taboo and may even be welcomed. Different tools and resources may need to be provided in training based on the power distance level of the culture. For instance, while all could benefit from a focus on ethical decision making and whistleblowing, higher power-distance countries may need additional training, resources, and support to facilitate the reporting of unethical behavior committed by those in positions of power. Additionally, educating employees about the potential effects of social pressures (e.g., authority figures) on their decision making may be even more important in countries with higher power distance. While these suggestions involve giving extra support to employees in higher power-distance countries, those in lower power-distance countries may benefit from ethics training content that focuses on the use of *appropriate* reporting channels and strategies for gathering more information about perceived ethical issues. Although individuals in low power-distance cultures may be more willing to report, they may not always be aware of the appropriate channels of communication or what information must be gathered prior to reporting an issue. Providing them with the tools on how to do this may be especially important.

Competitiveness

Competitiveness refers to the degree that members in a society work to get ahead or work together (Hofstede, 2001). Competitive cultures are assertive and focused primarily on achieving success and earning rewards. In comparison, collaborative cultures promote cooperation with a stronger emphasis on achieving consensus. For examples of collaborative cultures we can look to Denmark, Sweden, and Russia, and for competitive cultures we can look to South Africa, the USA, and Germany.

Employees in competitive cultures may be primarily interested in getting ahead and may place less of an emphasis on the interests of other stakeholders (Blodgett, Lu, Rose, & Vitell, 2001). When providing ethics training for individuals in competitive cultures, a pitch on the importance of ethics must align with their desire to compete and to win. Framing ethics as a competitive advantage or a differentiator may be important in this context (see Chapter 1). In the race to get ahead, those in competitive cultures may also be less willing to seek help from others and, therefore, ethics training may need to place a heavier emphasis on the importance of seeking help to effectively resolve dilemmas. It may also be important for ethics trainings to highlight that being the first to find a solution may not always be ideal in this case emphasizing the importance of taking time to work with others to generate and implement a solution may be appropriate. In contrast, those in collaborative cultures may have difficulty resolving a dilemma, as they may want to find a solution that satisfies everyone in the group. In many instances, this may not be possible. The notion that a resolution to an ethical dilemma may not satisfy everyone in the group may be difficult for those in a collaborative culture to accept. Employees in this culture may then benefit from practice activities (e.g., role play) focused on identifying and communicating effective solutions that may not satisfy everyone involved.

Long-term orientation

Long-term orientation focuses on the extent to which a society upholds long-standing traditions and views attempts for change skeptically (Hofstede, 2001). Individuals in a society that has more of a long-term orientation, such as South Korea, Switzerland, and Japan, tend to be persistent and prudent, with an eye toward future goals and rewards. They also likely view adaptability as an important trait in order to reach one's goals. Individuals in societies that are more short-term focused, such as New Zealand, Canada, and Nigeria, typically take more interest in maintaining the status quo, upholding tradition, and saving 'face.'

Employees in societies that are more short-term focused may find it difficult to make decisions that 'rock the boat' or go against the status quo. On the one hand, such stability in decision making can facilitate compliance with traditional values and norms. On the other hand, because organizations operate in complex and dynamic environments with changing rules and norms (see Chapter 11), short-term orientation may at times hinder ethical decision making in the face of novel situations. Research has suggested that this type of thinking in the extreme may be associated with less ethical decision making (Watts et al., 2020). With a long-term focused culture, a willingness to persist may help employees through tough ethical dilemmas that require sustained effort. Additionally, adaptability may also allow employees to shift with norms and regulations and make ethical decisions in accordance with them. However, persistence may result in what researchers refer to as, escalation of commitment, or the continued pursuit of a failing effort (Staw, 1981). You might think of it as the feeling that you are in too deep and it is too late to back out now. Escalation of commitment has been used to explain why some individuals commit unethical acts (Street & Street, 2006). Additionally, adapting to changes may be important, but shifting with the wind to achieve a long-term outcome may promote a mindset that any action is acceptable in order to obtain the future goal. This potential 'ends justify the means' attitude can certainly cause trouble, resulting in unethical decisions in pursuit of a bigger goal. Ethics training managers may want to emphasize the potential pitfalls in this thinking and provide strategies for being more adaptable to individuals in short-term oriented cultures and considering the consequences of one's short-term actions to those in long-term oriented cultures.

Indulgence

Indulgence represents the extent to which a society seeks gratification and pleasure. Highly indulgent societies, including Australia, the USA, and Venezuela, encourage fun and pleasure-seeking activities and show little restraint. In contrast, societies focused on restraint, such as China, Japan, and South Korea, tend to downplay gratification and place a greater emphasis on adhering to social norms.

When it comes to ethics training, presenting a traditional, heavily rule-focused ethics training program to members of a highly indulgent society may be met with resistance. Additionally, individuals in an indulgent culture might be tempted to ignore or quickly resolve an ethical dilemma so they can get back to the more fun things in life. After all, ethical dilemmas are typically not the most enjoyable experiences. When working in highly indulgent societies, ethics training managers may want to spend more time highlighting the importance of ethical dilemmas. This may help to drive home the point that even though it may not be enjoyable, avoiding or resolving the dilemma in a less than optimal way may result in more pain than if one had taken the time and effort to resolve it in the first place. Additionally, this group may especially benefit from a training experience that has a bit more fun incorporated through activities such as games and role plays. Alternatively, those in a more restrained culture may require a greater emphasis on how social rules and norms can play both a positive and negative role in their decision making. Similar to those in high power-distance cultures, individuals in restrained cultures may need a strong emphasis on the power of the situation and how following social norms may produce positive results if they are ethical, but may lead someone astray if they ignore other important perspectives and considerations. Adding activities that encourage employees in restrained cultures to consider how other stakeholders in different social groups with unique social norms may view their decision or behavior may be beneficial.

Although we highlight the potential influence of cultural dimensions on ethics training decisions, it does not mean that your ethics training program needs to be bound to a particular culture. It is important to remember that the statements made here are generalizations about cultures and that individual differences among trainees do exist. Additionally, not all trainees may be from that culture. In some instances, there may also be expatriates working outside of their home country. As such, force-fitting a culture-specific lens on ethics training could lead managers to miss the nuances of the trainees involved. Instead of redesigning training for each individual country or culture, ethics training managers should be aware of these differences and design or select training methods most appropriate for the cultural context, recognizing that some approaches or content may need to be re-framed or adjusted to reduce negative reactions of trainees and to help them incorporate the training content into their everyday work lives. Table 12.1 provides a summary of the impact of cultural differences on training design and implementation.

Implications for managers

The previous sections highlighted the specific impact of cultural dimensions on ethics training practices. However, broad implications may also be drawn regarding how culture impacts training design, implementation, and evaluation.

Table 12.1 Summary of Cultural Dimensions and Implications for Ethics Training

Cultural Dimension	Definition	Level	Implications
Individualism	The extent to which individuals take interest in the goals of a broader group compared to the goals of oneself alone	High	Provide activities that encourage processing of group outcomes
		Low	Provide activities that encourage processing of personally relevant outcomes
Uncertainty avoidance	The extent to which members of a society manage ambiguity, or the degree to which a culture will tolerate ambiguity	High	Use a compliance-based approach but emphasize tools for navigating ambiguity in ethical dilemmas
		Low	Focus on complexities of ethical dilemmas but provide support for understanding and applying rules
Power distance	The extent to which power is distributed within a society	High	Educate on social pressures; provide training, resources, and support on reporting unethical behavior and seeking help from supervisors
		Low	Provide information on strategies for gathering more information as well as *appropriate* reporting channels
Competitiveness	The extent to which a society is assertive and focused on achievement versus cooperation and consensus	High	Describe business ethics as a competitive advantage; encourage trainees to seek help
		Low	Emphasize that trainees may not be able to satisfy everyone with their decision; provide tools for communicating decisions that do not satisfy everyone
Long-term orientation	The extent to which a society upholds traditions and views change skeptically	High	Discuss the value of tradition
		Low	Discuss the value of adapting

(*continued on next page*)

Table 12.1 (*continued*)

Cultural Dimension	Definition	Level	Implications
Indulgence	The extent to which a society seeks gratification or pleasure	High	Add fun training activities; emphasize importance of making good decisions
		Low	Discuss the positives and negatives of adhering to social norms; include activities focused on other's views of their behavior

Training design and implementation

A global, one-size fits all approach to ethics training will likely not produce optimal results. Practically, when operating in isolation in different countries, this implies that a training developed for a US company may prove less effective in a Chinese, Indian, or Dutch company. The challenge increases, however, when large multinational or international companies wish to develop an ethics training program for their entire workforce. Tailored training approaches may be needed in each country to improve trainee reactions and develop content that will transfer to the local context after training. To do so, ethics training managers must familiarize themselves with local customs, perspectives, and laws prior to embarking on an ethics training effort.

For more information on the cultural personalities of specific countries, we suggest exploring The Hofstede Insights' Cultural Comparison Tool (www.hofstede-insights.com). This resource allows users to select a country, view where it falls along Hofstede's cultural dimensions, and make comparisons with other countries. This knowledge can then be used to understand how training design characteristics or approach may be altered from one culture to another.

Additionally, training managers must consider the unique experiences of expatriates and the ethical issues that may emerge when working in another culture. In this instance, including an ethics component in cultural awareness training prior to an assignment may prove valuable. In one study of Google's approach to cross-cultural ethics training in China, researchers identified six questions that can help facilitate ethical decision making among managers faced with ethical issues in unfamiliar territory (Hamilton, Knouse, & Hill, 2008). These questions are summarized as follows:

- What is the practice in question?
- What are the legal views on this practice?
- Do views on this practice differ by culture and if so, is it an ethical problem?
- What are the industry and organizational views on this practice?
- Is there room to influence practices in the host country?
- Can changing the practice improve market practices in the host country?

Further, Mary Gentile (2016) highlighted key steps ethics managers can take to successfully integrate ethics training programs across cultures. As she describes, when developing an ethics-focused program for entrepreneurs in Delhi, she faced skepticism from trainees. She remembers a trainee stating to her:

> Madam, we are very happy to have you here and we are happy to listen to what you have to say about ethics and values in the workplace. But this is India, and we are entrepreneurs—we can't even get a driver's license without paying a bribe.

This statement, a stark reminder of differences in the way businesses and workers operate across cultures, led Gentile to suggest several practical steps for ethics training managers:

1. *Recognize reality:* As we've emphasized throughout this chapter, it is important that ethics training managers understand the relevant culture and acknowledge the unique pressures and challenges for those working in those cultures.
2. *Start with respect:* Understand that trainees already have values but that their cultural context may make some of them more challenging to act upon, appeal to their own desire to behave in alignment with those values that researchers have found to be universal

('hyper-norms'), and emphasize that this training is about empowering them to do so.

3. *Provide emotional distance:* When using cases, ask trainees to respond as the characters (e.g., how could the protagonist act on their values?) as opposed to as themselves (e.g., what would you do?). This simple change can help trainees explore alternative options and feel more empowered about their action plan.

4. *Use real examples:* Sharing real, culturally relevant examples of how others have responded to ethical situations provides trainees with relevant role models and shows that others in this culture can act this way.

In addition to providing a way for ethics training managers to acknowledge the uniqueness of specific cultures, these steps also present an opportunity for trainees to reflect on their own values and behaviors. In turn, these steps encourage trainees to consider how their behavior aligns and misaligns with their values and provide a safe space for considering new behaviors and choices that best fit with the values they espouse. Lastly, these steps provide a framework for trainees to practice skills for enacting these values after leaving the training room.

Evaluation

Given that methods may vary in their impact across cultures, ethics training managers should carefully monitor the results of these efforts by culture. To do so, ethics training managers can analyze the results of ethics training by each country, or subregion separately. For example, if conducting training in the USA and China, ethics training managers should separate the data for each country, examining the results for both the USA and China distinctly. Doing so will provide insight into how the ethics training is working within the unique cultures. Although a full investigation into the underlying cause of the differences is warranted, ethics training managers should consider how the cultural differences at play may be impacting the results.

Additionally, some countries may be more or less willing to engage in the evaluation process itself. For instance, countries with a highly indulgent culture may not want to spend the time evaluating training outcomes. Further, if evaluation opportunities are offered in indulgent societies, employees may be less likely to take them. This may present a unique challenge for ethics training managers who are trying to evaluate the success of their programs. In addition to the strategies regarding planning for evaluation challenges discussed in Chapter 10, ethics training managers may also consider how they frame evaluation processes in these countries to encourage more participation and secure buy-in from senior-level management.

Lastly, it may be possible that some countries will be less willing to recognize and share results if the results do not paint leaders, or themselves, in a positive light. For example, ethics training managers and others involved in ethics training efforts in high power-distance cultures may be reluctant to share negative training results with their supervisors, especially in the case where a senior leader has spearheaded the effort. Those in competitive cultures may see negative results as failing and may be tempted to hide results from others to avoid tainting their reputation and chances of advancement. We challenge ethics training managers to be as transparent as possible with results across cultures to encourage further development of the training efforts and improvement (see Chapter 6).

Conclusion

Although this chapter presents many ideas regarding how cultural differences may impact the design and effectiveness of ethics training efforts, many of these claims are speculative. At the time of this writing, very few research studies have directly investigated the implications of cultural differences for ethics training.

However, culture clearly plays a large role in how individuals may perceive, interpret, and respond to ethical issues. These cultural differences can then influence how trainees react to and what they learn from ethics training efforts. Additionally, legal differences between countries will dictate behavioral standards and expectations, which will influence what content may be presented around the world. Ethics training managers must then be aware of both legal and cultural differences when working internationally.

As globalization continues, the issue of cross-cultural ethics training will only continue to increase in importance. We hope that the contents of this book help prepare ethics training managers to lead the way, world-wide, in the effort to create a more ethical future for business and beyond.

References

Becker, H., & Fritzsche, D. J. (1987). Business ethics: A cross-cultural comparison of managers' attitudes. *Journal of Business Ethics*, 6, 289–295.

Blodgett, J. G., Lu, L. C., Rose, G. M., & Vitell, S. J. (2001). Ethical sensitivity to stakeholder interests: A cross-cultural comparison. *Journal of the Academy of Marketing Science*, 29, 190–202.

Butler, S. (January 21, 2019). Why are wages so low for garment workers in Bangladesh? *The Guardian*. Retrieved on January 31, 2020 from https://www.theguardian.com/business/2019/jan/21/low-wages-garment-workers-bangladesh-analysis.

Chinese Culture Connection. (1987). Chinese values and the search for culture-free dimensions of culture. *Journal of Cross-Cultural Psychology*, 18, 143–164.

Christie, P. M. J., Kwon, I. G., Stoeberl, P. A., & Baumhart, R. (2003). A cross-cultural comparison of ethical attitudes of business managers: India, Korea, and the United States. *Journal of Business Ethics*, 46, 263–287.

Davis, M. A., Johnson, N. B., & Ohmer, D. G. (1998). Issue-contingent effects on ethical decision making: A cross-cultural comparison. *Journal of Business Ethics*, 17, 373–389.

Forsyth, D. R. (1980). A taxonomy of ethical ideologies. *Journal of Personality and Social Psychology*, 39, 175–184.

Gentile, M. C. (December 23, 2016). Talking about ethics across cultures. *Harvard Business Review*. Retrieved on June 2, 2020 from https://hbr.org/2016/12/talking-about-ethics-across-cultures.

Hamilton, J. B., Knouse, S. B., & Hill, V. (2008). Google in China: A manager-friendly heuristic model for resolving cross-cultural ethical conflicts. *Journal of Business Ethics*, 86, 143–157.

Hofstede, G. (1980). *Culture's consequences: International differences in work-related values*. Beverly Hills, CA: Sage.

Hofstede, G. (2001). *Culture's consequences: Comparing values, behaviors, institutions and organizations across nations*. Thousand Oaks, CA: Sage.

Hofstede, G. (2002). The pitfalls of cross-national survey research: A reply to the article by Spector et al. on the psychometric properties of the Hofstede Values Survey Module 1994. *Applied Psychology: An International Review*, 51(1), 170–173.

Hofstede, G., Hofstede, G. J., & Minkov, M. (2010). *Cultures and organizations: Software of the mind* (3rd ed.). New York, NY: McGraw-Hill.

Husted, B. W., & Allen, D. B. (2008). Toward a model of cross-cultural business ethics: The impact of individualism and collectivism on the ethical decision-making process. *Journal of Business Ethics, 82*, 293–305.

International Commissioner's Office (2020). *Guide to the general data protection regulation (GDPR)*. Retrieved on January 31, 2020 from https://ico.org.uk/for-organisations/guide-to-data-protection/guide-to-the-general-data-protection-regulation-gdpr/.

Richert, J., Benello, J. P., & Bognar, S. (2019). *American Factory [Motion picture]*. United States: Higher Ground Productions and Participant Media. January 25.

Right Management (June 4, 2013). Many managers found to fail in overseas assignments. Retrieved on January 31, 2020 from https://www.manpowergroup.com/wcm/connect/right-cn-zh/home/thoughtwire/categories/media-center/Many+Managers+Found+to+Fail+in+Overseas+Assignments.

Stajkovic, A., & Luthans, F. (1997). Business ethics across cultures: A social cognitive model. *Journal of World Business, 32*, 17–34.

Staw, B. M. (1981). The escalation of commitment to a course of action. *Academy of Management Review, 6*, 577–587.

Street, M., & Street, V. L. (2006). The effects of escalating commitment on ethical decision-making. *Journal of Business Ethics, 64*, 343–356.

Transparency International UK (n.d.). *The Bribery Act*. Retrieved on June 2, 2020 from https://www.transparency.org.uk/our-work/business-integrity/bribery-act/.

Universal Declaration of Human Rights. (1948). Accessed on January 30, 2020 from https://www.un.org/en/universal-declaration-human-rights/.

United Nations (1948). *The universal declaration of human rights*. Retrieved on January 31, 2020 from https://www.ohchr.org/documents/publications/guidingprinciplesbusinesshr_en.pdf.

United Nations (2011). *Guiding principles on business and human rights: Implementing the United Nations "Protect, Respect, and Remedy" framework*.

Retrieved on January 31, 2020 from https://www.ohchr.org/documents/publications/guidingprinciplesbusinesshr_en.pdf.

Watts, L. L., Medeiros, K. E., McIntosh, T. J., & Mulhearn, T. J. (2020). *Decision biases in the context of ethics: Initial scale development and validation. Personality & Individual Differences, 153(15)*, 1- 13. doi:10.1016/j.paid.2019.109609.

Weaver, G. R. (2001). Ethics programs in global businesses: Culture's role in managing ethics. *Journal of Business Ethics, 30*, 3–15.

APPENDIX

CALCULATING COHEN'S *D*

Cohen's d is a standardized measure of effect size that can be used to evaluate the effectiveness of ethics training programs (see Chapter 3). Cohen's d can be calculated using the following formula:

$$Cohen's\ d = \frac{(M_2 - M_1)}{Pooled\ SD}$$

In this formula, 'M' stands for mean and 'SD' stands for standard deviation. The mean is the average of a set of scores. Notice that there are two means in this formula—one for each set of scores. By subtracting one mean from the other mean, we get an estimate of the raw difference between the two sets of scores. We use the word 'raw' here to indicate that the difference has not yet been standardized.

To standardize the difference between the means, we need to divide the raw difference in means by the pooled standard deviation. Each set of scores has its own standard deviation, or the average distance between each score within a set and the mean score of that set. There are six steps to calculating the standard deviation of a set of scores.

1. Calculate the mean of the set.
2. Subtract the mean from each score to get difference scores.

3. Square each difference score (this forces all of the difference scores to be positive).
4. Add up the difference scores.
5. Divide the sum by the number of scores in the sample minus one.
6. Take the square root.

Note that these steps need to be followed twice, once for each set of scores. Then, the pooled standard deviation can be calculated using the following formula, in which 'SD$_1$' and 'SD$_2$' represent the standard deviations calculated from the first and second set of scores:

$$Pooled\ SD = \sqrt{\frac{(SD_1^2 + SD_2^2)}{2}}$$

Means and standard deviations can, of course, be calculated by hand, but it's far easier to use Microsoft Excel or other basic data analysis programs. There are also many free websites that can help you calculate Cohen's d. Check out the R *Psychologist* website by Kristoffer Magnusson (https://rpsychologist.com/d3/cohend/) to use a free interactive Cohen's d visualization tool.

Reference

Magnusson, K. (n.d.). Interpreting Cohen's *d* effect size: An interactive visualization. R *Psychologist*. Retrieved on July 31, 2019, at: https://rpsychologist.com/d3/cohend/.

INDEX

Printed in the United States
By Bookmasters